Her Life…
Behind Closed
Doors

Her Life…
Behind Closed Doors

Christian Foster- Bates

Her Life…Behind Closed Doors/ by Christian Foster- Bates
ISBN-13:
978-0692669051 (Foster Girl Productions)

ISBN-10:
0692669051
Order copies
Email fostergirlproductions@gmail.com or www.fostergirlproductions.org
Questions or Comments hlbcdinfo@gmail.com
Printed in the United States of America

Cover Design: www.fostergirlproductions.org

This book recounts events in the life of Christian Foster-Bates according to author's perspective. All stories are true, some names and identifying details have been changed to protect the privacy of those involved.

Unless otherwise indicated scripture quotations identified are from King James Version & New International Version of the bible.

Thank you to each and every friend and associate who never bashed me for living a double lifestyle and accepting me as is.

Mom although you did not condone the lifestyle I once lived, I thank you so much for never kicking me out of the house or disowning me. I love you and my family with all my heart.

To my spiritual mother and mentor Robin McKnight thank you for sharing your testimony with me and showing me that overcoming homosexuality is possible.

Thank you to my wonderful Husband Kevin Bates, for sticking by me through the journey and process of writing this book. I thank God for saving you for me until I was fully free. I could not imagine life without you.

God, those personal talks we've had and those many nights I struggled and wanted to give in. So many times, I did give up and went back into sin. You allowed for me to have a way of escape like you said in your word. You kept me when I did not want to be kept. You saved me when I did not want to be saved. I love you, Jesus, and I thank you for saving my soul and as a promise from me to you, I will spread the gospel and share my testimony with everyone.

Contents

INTRODUCTION

Through the eyes of a praying mother

One night my mom attended a revival at New Day Church in Beaumont. As service was ending, she proceeded to walk to the offering table and drop her money into the basket, while holding me.

There standing was a very short, older woman in her late 80s. My mom said she'd never seen this woman a day in her life. As she was walking off and approached her seat to hear the benediction, the elderly woman quickly stood up with authority.

Pointing to me, she said such profound words; "That baby is going to be greatly used by God! She's gonna draw a lot of young people to Christ, and she's not someone who will be ashamed to tell people about God! She's going to be prosperous."

Twenty five years later it's safe to say that this word is definitely a prophetic word that has already begun through God's will.

DIVINE ENCOUNTER
5 years later

Flipping the light switch, my mom carries me from the living room to my room and tucks me into my twin sized day-bed. As she began to walk down the hallway to her room, she hears something unusual. "The Enemy is going to try and put a lesbian spirit on her." My mom, startled and confused, said she stopped dead in her tracks. She heard these words so clearly from God.

My interpretation of this was God forewarning my mom of what she would have to begin to pray for. God will give you warning before destruction, but it is up to us to stay prayed up and always cover ourselves with the Blood of Jesus.

"Don't let the devil turn your curiosity into an addiction. If you know it's wrong, then don't even test the waters."

-Marcus Stanley

This book recounts events in the life of Christian Foster-Bates according to author's perspective. All stories are true, some names and identifying details have been changed to protect the privacy of those involved.

1

Behind Closed Doors

Now let's move forward. I wanted you all to have a glimpse of my life before I first came onto this Earth. You will later discover that unlike others, I myself did not seek an alternative lifestyle because I did not have my dad around, I definitely did not seek this forbidden lifestyle because someone forced me. I came from a loving family, and was raised in church. I bet you're baffled already right? *Well how did you get into the homosexual lifestyle, Christian? Please tell me!* Slow down. I have to give you the full layout and blue-print of my life, starting with my childhood.

In some awkward, crafty way the enemy took his best shot. It did not kill me, but residue from the gun powder would later begin to seep through my skin. I had the opportunity to pass multiple tests from

God; however, I would allow for the curiosity of my emotions to take over. I failed my first test, which would change my life forever, simply by a decision to test my own curiosity.

This would become the beginning of many suicide attempts, multiple heart breaks, bad dreams that turned into reality, car accidents, losing my mind and experiencing near death. No one knew that I would master covering pain so well by becoming the support system of others. No one would know that I was blaming everyone internally by being put on a pedestal. I had a mental perception that everyone was obligated to cater to me. Helping others with their personal issues would put me in position to cover up what I was dealing with. We as humans like to use validation from others as our confirmation, but when God sends a sign or confirmation we ignore it and go to everyone for opinions, even when God has clearly stated facts. Of course, we have to make excuses as to why we do things and live a certain way.

I was somewhat envious of those who received the backlash, negativity and condemning comments, because I needed proof to know that what I was doing was not okay. I wanted human contact as confirmation. I never received that correction through human contact, almost as if people avoided hurting my feelings with the truth. I was everyone's advice giver, sister, friend, prayer partner, and "go to" person. Oddly enough, I wanted that hatred so that I could change who I chose to be. I would eventually turn my back on God and, consider becoming an atheist while attempting to plan an engagement, but you would never know because all of this was...behind closed doors.

2

Planting Unknown Seeds

Growing up I wasn't as fortunate enough to have siblings around, but that void would later be replaced by those whom I would become connected with. As a child I was hyperactive and tried to stay busy. I recall always being chased by dogs, playing basketball, climbing trees, and hiding my neighbors' shoes under their porch. My mom made sure I was surrounded by God's Word by always attending church. I was teased a lot and asked the same repetitive questions as to why was I spending so much time in church.

Even until this day, my mother serves as a perfect example of what it is to be Christ like. I was never shown a reason to stray away from God. Her faith, and true relationship with God was the best example a child could ask for. That was one of many seeds that was planted in my life.

My mom enrolled me into Greater Good Hope Child Development Center, a private school in my hometown of Beaumont. I was a very mischievous child. I would take classmates lunches, and hide the evidence, but I always got caught! I cheated on many tests and got caught! I stole and got caught! I seemed to always make my way into the principal's office. I'm sure my mom dreaded coming to get me, thinking *what did you do now Christian?*

One girl in my kindergarten class would also get in to trouble, just like me so we would be set apart during naptime, in order for the teachers to keep an eye on us. One afternoon, while we were laughing and playing she proceeded to act as if she was having sex on her mat. I like to tell parents all the time, your children know more than you think. As I watched her, I knew what was going on because around this age I had viewed a couple of sex scenes from various movies. I thought of it as a joke, and I began to play along and do the same. I became a gardener watering my own unknown seeds.

By this time, my dad was not around, and the only two memories I had of him would replay as I got older. The first was him leaving our home, and at the age of four he showed up to a birthday party of mine walking into the house with a cowboy hat on.

My cousins Eric, Jacob & JP were considered my brothers, so I would enjoy hanging with them whenever I could. We played every type of game system you could think of. Sega Dreamcast, Game Cube, all the Play Stations, Nintendo 64 and so forth. When we weren't playing video games they would wrestle me, or we would just play basketball all day and race in the street. Their friends always came over, and with me being the only girl around, they would let me play basketball with them, which developed my athletic ability and love for basketball.

Growing up as an only child, my mom didn't support me in me spending the night at others' homes, even if we knew them, and if it did happen it was very rare. I only wanted to be accompanied by kids my age to have fun and occupy my time. I recall going over to one friend's house for an all-girls sleepover one summer. As we all began preparing for bed, we gathered our pillows, blankets, sleeping bags and laid out in the living room. As small conversations began to take place, without thought or hesitation, I got on top of each girl, doing what I had done in naptime. I begin to hump them. Some may have reason to believe that this sort of act would be considered playful, but that's where we all go wrong even in our own lives. We dabble into all types of activities with lack of knowledge or even full knowledge just see how far we can go. You begin to plant seeds that slowly manifest in your life over the course of time. You thought that that seed never grew or that plant died but as you continue to go through life you will have a full plant and wonder how it got there. The girls at the sleepover all laughed and one person said "you're gay" and we laughed even more. I thought it was funny, just as they all thought and I laid back down and we never spoke of it again even as we all got older that day was put to rest. I didn't realize that just acting out one simple thing that seemed so playful, would lead to my own curiosity. I planted an unknown seed in the atmosphere, which produced and birthed even more spirits that began to manifest one being an addiction to pornography later on.

3

Preparation & Transition

At the age of seven, I accepted Jesus as my personal savior, and not because I was forced into doing so. I remember one Sunday after church, I was in the kitchen playing and I started thinking about where I would go, if I died. So I asked my mom the simple question "Will I go to Heaven?" and being the straight forward person she is, she replied, "If you accept Jesus as your personal savior, then yes!" I was very smart for my age, so I understood everything she told me. I left out of her room that day went back to the kitchen, and I prayed to God. I asked him come into my heart and save me. I ultimately said this to God because I didn't want to die and go to Hell, I felt that saying that prayer was good enough for me. There are many people that may wonder why Christians believe in man that we cannot see and put our trust into him. If you are one of these people that may have been wondering well I have a simple answer for you. All it takes is one encounter for you to have with Jesus Christ to change your life forever. In various ways, by miracle, his presence, utterance and so forth.

That one prayer that took place that day would change the way I seen things for the rest of my life. I was able to tap into another viewing seeing things through a spiritual realm, not only the natural. From that moment on, I would go into our laundry room and see a black spirit lingering. It was tall and was positioned near the corner each time I passed by. I never told my mom because I wasn't afraid, and a lot of times I mostly ignored it.

When I was in the second grade my mom had one and one only conversation with me about having sex before marriage. Our first conversation was straight to the point. (As if I already had a clear definition prior to our conversation and she was giving a final review) *"Christian don't have sex, you should wait until you're married"* and that was that. Those words stuck with me ever since. I had in my mind that I would remain a virgin until I was married. I never questioned it, my theory on this whole wait to marriage thing was to wait so that I wouldn't get pregnant that was my take on it.

As an only child, I was taught a lot early on. Most people assume that if you're an only child that you must be spoiled, but that wasn't true at least not in my position. Being raised in a single parent household my mom worked at night while my grandma, "Chocolate Grams" as I call her, would watch me. I spent many nights looking out of the window, as my mom pulled out the driveway and headed to SAMs. Since I did not have any siblings, I did whatever I could to entertain myself. Played with my Barbie dolls, went outside played basketball, snuck over to my neighbor's house. I would even go as far as just running through the house, accidently breaking something and figuring out how I could hide what I'd just done. One day I decided to go into the laundry room and sit on the floor for absolutely no reason. There sat a gallon of bleach so I grabbed it and studied the bottle. Twisting open the blue cap looking inside I heard something say *drink it.* Sometimes if I was just to look inside the bottle I would hear that same voice say *put it in your eyes.* That spirit that was in our laundry room would follow us from each house we moved into, and I later was able to interpret it as the Spirit of Death. So imagine the Grim Reaper following you to each house. Yes, creepy I know!

My imagination had already begun to run wild, so it was never hard for me to entertain myself. I would easily become bored, playing with my Barbie dolls or a basketball so my grandma just purchased a new computer around this time and I would always get on different websites. Checking out the most current rappers Lil' Romeo & Lil' Bow Wow, sometimes just going on Nickelodeon and Disney website. At the time a family member of mind was oversees and his mail would come to the house we were living at. One day I saw a Playboy magazine come through the mail. Curiosity begin to set in and each month a new magazine was rolling in. One day I just had to see what it was all about and why there was a new woman on the front of the cover each month. Sneaking off to another part of the house I unwrapped the plastic and begin to look at nude women in these magazines finding it very interesting and entertaining. Not able to keep the magazines long I had to quickly return them to where I would originally find them so no one would know I opened them. Still in elementary I dabbled into masturbation because of the thoughts that ran through my mind. Not only from the Playboy magazines, but having access to the computer at home, thinking about different guys at school. I didn't know if this was bad or not but a part of my spirit felt convicted in what I was partaking in along with embarrassment at such a young age. I know you may be reading this and may think yea that's normal I did that or I do that now. Well the bible clearly states that your body is a temple unto God and it does not belong to you. People see masturbation as a way of pleasing themselves or a quick thrill or releasing a feeling, but you must look at the bigger picture. What door have you opened just from masturbating? Are you now addicted? Do you now desire to sleep with someone instead of pleasing yourself? Are you already sleeping with others to fulfil your quick desire for a moment? Let's break it down. Masturbation can form many spirits, Addiction, lusting after another human whom is not your spouse, depression, loneliness, confusion. Even anger no telling what spirits you have now allowed into your house and that's just to name a few. Discipline requires sacrifice and in order for you to stop what is not in the will of God you must discipline your spirit and kill out your flesh. Ask yourself would I do this in front of God if he was visible at this very moment? That will let you know off top that it's not his will for you.

A few years later we ended up moving and the same dark spirit that I'd seen in the wash room traveled with us. Now in middle school adjusting to new friends, I adapted to a new interest of watching porn. When everyone went to sleep or off to their rooms I would stay up in the living room watching different channels that offered what I wanted to see. I had just tapped into a new realm not even realizing what effect this could potentially have on me. Showtime, Starz, HBO, and Encore you name it I probably watched it on that channel. Only barely a teenager I had become addicted to pornography. It was always men and women on the screen, but I had become bored with what I was watching and didn't care to see the opposite sex engage into sexual activities. I ended up finding a regular show that was based around the homosexual community. I begin to like the show not even realizing that I just opened a second door. First was pornography now I'd just tapped into the homosexual world at a distance. Originally I liked the show just because I thought it was good. Liking what I had saw it started with me taking an interest to seeing two women together and later seeing just men together. Another door had open and this time the spirit of perversion and confusion attached itself to me. I even went as far as creating an account on *Tagged*, a form of social media at the time portraying myself as a guy. I had stolen someone's picture offline and added it to become my profile picture. I was catfishing someone before MTV even created the show years to come. I remember the one girl in particular I messaged, she was brown skinned and seemed so happy that I had messaged her, so now I lead to the question of *will you be my girlfriend*. My imagination was running wild I had begun to imagine what her expressions and actions were at that very moment. This went on for maybe a day or two, possibly even longer until I told her that I was really a girl and shortly after I deleted my account. I just remember being in pain after I had told her I was a girl, but deep down inside I somewhat wanted to become a boy. This was all preparation and transition into another life. Meaning I just sowed another seed, planted it, and watered it. Once it grew the devil was getting ready to hand deliver flowers to my door step.

One day my mom and I were in Home Depot, and I felt so embarrassed just thinking about how I had become addicted to pornography and masturbation, I told God, *"Please show my mom what I'm going through so she can pray for me"*.

You have to get to a point in your struggle that if you want help as bad as you say you do, you will do what you have to do to get help, even if it means exposing yourself. You must be willing to strip your flesh and cut your dead skin off in order to reach your full potential. Under all of that dead weight God is trying to help you get to your full potential, but you have to meet him half way. We are so consumed with what the world is doing that we start to think exactly like those who have no relationship with God or halfway have one. When you begin to think and act like the world you eventually become the world. At that age I, knew how to talk to God and ask for help, but I wasn't sure how to strip my flesh of the dead weight I had begun to carry.

Now in the seventh grade I'd met this guy name Robert who would become my first boyfriend, we met in the only class we had together which was P.E. There were mixed grades in our class. Some of the school's best girl basketball players attended that class with us. I wanted so badly to become their friend and dress like them. At the time basketball was my passion and seeing them play, cross people up, and run fast as I did attracted me. I wanted so badly to be like them that I begin to like them, forming a physical attraction. I would often take note of how they dressed. There was just something different about the way they carried themselves. The following school year we ended up moving once again which meant Robert and I would break up.

Transitioning into eighth grade, I switched schools attending Vincent Middle School so I decided to try out for basketball. When I made the team I became the starting point guard. Our Coach would call us by our last name's and that's where "Foster" originated from and people would soon begin to call me that from now on, some even thought that was my first name.

Between the 7th and 8th graders I had friends who were on the team that dressed in a way that I desired to. In my eyes, they were all so pretty but the way they dressed opened the door for me to try something new. I knew something felt different. In an odd way I couldn't understand the way I was feeling if I liked them or just liked the way they dressed or both. I wanted to be like them, because they played basketball well and yet had a masculine demeanor about them, but yet they were still feminine. I didn't realize the way I carried myself was already duplicating the things I saw on a daily basis. I was looking in a mirror each and every day at others, not noticing that I was looking back at myself. I was now mentally preparing myself for a transtion that I had no idea was about to take place. We had to wear uniforms so my daily outfits were tennis shoes, collar shirts and khaki shorts that went to my knees. I started thinking to much about what new things that I wanted to try and that carried over into my dreams. Not a very long one at all but I recall having a males private parts instead of my own. I remember waking up sad the next morning because It was no longer there, the idea of being a boy at the time was something that I begin to have desires for.

BOOM! That is where I failed at! I didn't have anyone to talk to about this at that time in my life but maybe you are in that position now. Your're reading your outlet now. Your desires should line up with God's desires for you. Well maybe you are one of those people that will quote the scripture *"God will give you the desires of your heart"*. You are totally correct but when your desires contradict the word of God that does not line up with his desires and basically your deleting the will that he has already printed out for your life. Maybe you feel like your are too young and you don't know where to start. Listen you are NEVER to young to take back your life. Spirits can snatch anyone up at anytime at any age. First and foremost start by covering your mind. Meaning get in your bible. Search scriputres that pertain to the mind and your situation. We make excuses as to not having a source when we really mean *I have a source it's the bible, but I don't want read I want someone to talk to me directly that is a human being.* That's fine but THE WORD OF GOD WILL KEEP YOU IN PERFECT PEACE. I would find out later on that my outlet had to be in through the word of God. As soon as you take that step of taking control of your mind, things will line up.

4

Get Me Out!

Entering into high school everything was so new. I was attending Central Medical Magnet High School, and I didn't know anyone. Originally, I planned on going to Westbrook High School, where people from my two previous middle schools would attend, but my heart longed to go to Ozen High School to pursue track.

By this time, I was dressing the part of what I had seen in middle school, not realizing that I already looked "gay". This is when I started off innocently, with small compliments, I would think, but never say. "She's pretty," or "I like her hair today." Attaching my thoughts to my current hidden feelings.

During my time in high school I would soon be approached by a woman who was in her twenties. Though I saw girls here and there, for the most part, I wasn't interested in dating a female more so because of my Christian beliefs or so I thought. This older women, Courtney, made me feel so good every time we were together or just communicating. She was someone I'd known pretty much all of my life but it wasn't until this school year when things transpired because of our constant communication. She offered something that I longed for and that was companionship, love, and an emotional connection. I had few boyfriends prior to her but it was a different type of feeling that I experienced. I liked a guy for himself which was gradual and I liked Courtney because of an emotional connection. What made things more comfortable was that she attended my church at that time so I trusted her.

This is an example of attracting various spirits by the way you carry yourself. Typically a spirit does not attract itself to something it cannot see. Think of it this way, imagine a coach with nine of the best swimmers but one is not as good as the others. What purpose would the swimmer serve if he is no better than the others? The coach sees potential on the inside of that young swimmer and wants to birth out something in him or her. Same way with evil spirits they want to birth out whatever they see in you, or whatever you feed your attention to, but your goal is to fight back through the blood of Jesus Christ and The Word of God. We intentionally and sometimes unknowingly allow for ourselves to be drawn in by whatever feels good, to truly find out if this is what God has for us or not, without consulting God first. The Bible says in your ways acknowledge him and he will direct your path, but we do things on our own as always.

The more the school year played out, I slowly fell into the

lifestyle. I felt trapped, mentally and I wanted someone to get me out! This feeling was equivalent to claustrophobia for me. The feeling of my flesh holding down my spirit-man felt so new and but unbearable at the same time.

Later that school year, I had the pleasure of meeting my dad for the first time in eleven years. We met at a track meet in Houston, which was where he happened to reside. I felt like I was introducing myself to a complete stranger. Oddly enough, it felt so good seeing him, beyond old pictures of us from my infancy. I figured I could give him a shot at being my dad, but this would only be the beginning of hope that turned into false realization. He began to walk in and out of my life. The years went by and I couldn't understand how someone who claimed to love me would never make time to see me. I tried to not make him exist in my mind, as if my mom had conceived me alone. It was as if I didn't know he was on Earth.

I now had the desire to want to be with another female, I felt an attraction and I always knew I wanted to give whomever I was with the love that I desired. What felt natural would soon become repeated patterns of depression that would replay for almost the next decade of my life.

At that time in my life, I wasn't the type to give people multiple chances, so I wasn't going to make an exception for my dad. He failed as a parent overall in my eyes, and I wanted nothing to do with him. Strange enough, I let go of grudges easily, along with people, and at that moment I knew I was done with my father.

So far gone into this new relationship I had fallen hard for Courtney during the school year. People say if you really want help you're going to do everything in your power to get it. I reached out to a couple of women at my church who prayed for me. After suffering and hiding this for some time now, I just wanted (and needed) a way out. They all stood next to me at the altar and begin to intercede for my deliverance. In order for a person to change you must be ready and you must want it. No one can "pray the gay away". You are going to have do a little more than just having others praying for you. Bluntly saying so that's just the reality of it.

We see things through the natural eye, but if we only really knew what was taking place in the spiritual realm, we would be more cautious of the way we took God for granted. I remained there for a moment, but something on the inside of me did not want the help nor the prayer. The devil was not happy that I was searching for the help I needed because this would ultimately ruin his initial goal taking my life. But Jesus said, "I have come that you may have life and have it more abundantly."

The devil began to fight against the prayers. I didn't say anything, make a scene, or say goodbye. I just walked away. I guess I didn't want it as badly as I thought because that night did not represent freedom, and I remained behind closed doors.

At that point in my life, I was in the baby stages and had time to come out from behind the closed door and lock it forever.

What people fail to realize is admitting you have a

stronghold is the first step to deliverance. You have to know that what you're doing in your heart is wrong, and not because someone else said it. Even if you believe that it's not a sin ask God, he is not the author of confusion and he has the final say. Personal feelings and Gods final say are two different things.

I truly believe people are afraid of truth. I wanted answers, so I did my own research based off my own personal conviction. Conviction is the Holy Spirit letting you know that you are not correct in your doing. You may feel convicted or feel bad because you know that what you're doing is wrong or goes against what you have been taught or moral feeling. No one ever came up to me and said, "Christian you know being gay is a sin and you're going to Hell". I have heard preachers speak against it, but I had to go into depth as to why it was so bad if I loved someone this much. I made up in my mind that I hated the depression that came along with having feelings for the same sex. So imagine how God felt, he loves us but hates the sin. We really have to stop overriding our gut feelings. Entering and engaging into this lifestyle at this time was the worse encounter ever.

When God sees greater in you he will not allow for you live comfortably without showing you signs, allowing for people to post a Facebook status, preach a sermon, even if you're on snapchat and someone happens to post a random ten second video on what you're going through. God doesn't have to try hard to grab your attention. Even you reading this book you may have thought "Hmm… I'll get this book because it looks like a good read" but little do you know I declare and decree that by the time you finish reading this book that you will be able to begin your deliverance process or be delivered and set free from whatever you are battling once you close the last page In Jesus Name.

A stronghold is a type of thinking pattern, based on lies and deception of the devil. Think of it as burglar bars on the windows of a house. You can't sneak out at night because your dad has the keys to the lock, therefore you are stuck and locked away in your room. You could go through your bedroom door, but we as humans tend to take the hard way out. The word of God says "For every temptation I have made a way of escape." That door to your bedroom is your escape however, we are hard-headed and still want to sneak out of the window. This applies to homosexuality or any sin.

In order to break free from the stronghold you must get the keys from your Father in heaven and let him pull you out like it is your last life-line. God has already made it plain to not be afraid or dismayed by the problem, because the battle is not yours, it's his. He gives you the battles as a test, to make you stronger so that you may help others. Don't question his authority, and remember, your pain is never in vain.

Several months later I attended Spiritual Encounter at Bishop IV Hilliard's, New Light Church in Houston, Texas. Pastor Preashea Hilliard and Pastor Irishea Hilliard were hosting a conference every year for youth and young adults. At that time, I was still dating Courtney, and I was considered as "undercover" or "in the closet." My most common attire at that time was from Ralph Lauren. I would often wear a ribbon to show some type of straight, feminine quality, despite my choice of clothing. However, my outward appearance would capture your eye faster than some one dollar, beauty supply ribbon. My heart grabbed on to the pain of not being able to tell anybody that I was having these feelings. I could really only take so much! I couldn't deal with not being able to tell anybody, friends nor family.

Be it homosexuality or any issue that you face, I encourage you to reach out to someone that you can trust and allow them to mentor you and get you to the correct people that can lead you to God, who will give you peace in your situation. After holding in that hurt, pain, bitterness, temptation, fear, and lies, you want to be at peace at the end of the day. Don't take it for granted when you feel as though someone is talking about your sin or struggle more than the other. That could just mean God is grabbing your attention. Typically when we are facing an issue we feel as though everyone is out to get us and targeting us. Not true! Everything is just timing, a person could speak on an issue that has nothing to do with us but as soon as one of our sins or struggles is brought up we tend to *go off* or give that person a piece of our mind out of anger. If you know that what you are doing is wrong please do not shoot the messenger for stepping on your toes. Could it just be that if that had not said something that God could be holding them accountable for not speaking up? Really take a step back and think about it.

One of Lucifer's top goals (and he has many top goals) is to have you losing sleep at night, because that opens another door for stress to come in, which will lead to slacking on the job or lower grades, even relationship problems. So you see, by holding in one thing even if it doesn't seem like a big deal, in actuality, it affects you and the people around you. It could even lead you to attempted suicide. Get the help that you need reach out to someone before it's too late.

Before I attended spiritual encounter there was this one friend I could talk to about anything. My best friend, Patricia, was always there for me. It was somewhat easier for me to explain to her what I was feeling without getting backlash and a list of questions. She made me feel comfortable, not enough for me to accept that lifestyle, but just knowing I had someone there to listen to me. Verbally expressing to someone felt so good, I just wanted to feel free, but God says "Cast your cares upon me" which I didn't. I would soon put my cares upon other's and eventually just sweep my own problems behind that closed door, which was quickly piling up with dust, trash, anger, lust, hate and the list goes on.

During one particular experience I had at Spiritual Encounter I cried out, I said "God help me, I don't want to be like this!" For the very first time in my life, I received the spirit of utterance which is a form of tongues. I remember seeing teens my age and young adults worshiping God having fun, enjoying the conference, and I thought to myself, *I want to do this.* I really want to live my life to the fullest for God without these extra feelings. However, slowly but surely, I fell back into the same dark path as I straddled the fence each time. It's easy to get into sin, it's also easy getting out of sin, but the real struggle is staying out and away from sin. We are born into sin, but it's our job as believers of Christ to repent and turn.

We desire to want to stop doing drugs, lying, sleeping around, beating on our loved ones, cheating, masturbating, thinking of killing someone, molesting a child, raping random women, being afraid, gossiping, throwing shade, stealing, hating or anything to please our flesh, but if we are truthful, could it be that our desire is blocked by our own thoughts and what we hold in our heart? The Bible says "For as a man thinketh in his heart so is he". If you have two desires in your heart one will eventually outweigh the other. You can't choose to love God, but still have other fleshly desires. You have to take that step on your own to make some type of change. That is the least that you owe God if you say love him and want to live for him.

Once the conference was over and we headed back to Beaumont, God began to show me that I have to want this for myself. He wanted to help but nothing is going to be handed to me. This is when free will came into play. God allows for us to live the way we like however, free will comes with consequences. God loves us so much that if he really wanted to, he could make us love him, but he's not like that at all; he gives us a choice.

Throughout high school, I still had many boyfriends. If I dated a guy it was because genuinely I liked them, but nine times out of ten, I always lost interest in them. Most people assumed that dating guys was used as a cover-up to hide my sexual preference, but that was never the case with me. I either liked you, or I didn't. Though I dressed the way I did, guys seemed to be attracted to me even more and this allowed me to be comfortable in my choice of clothing.

A new school year finally approached itself and here and a tall, skinny, light skinned guy took an interest in me. Due to all the girls that often approached him, you would never be able to tell, because of how shy he was. Jake was very persistent in getting me to be his girlfriend. Looking from the outside, I didn't want to deal with the girls that gravitated toward him.

Some of the athletes from the school traveled to Baylor University for a Christian Sports camp. There I would find myself caught in an act of pretending to be someone I wasn't. I wasn't even sure who I was. Somehow I got placed with the basketball girls as a mix-up. This was very odd because I was only running track in high school.

Though at my high school many girls were gay but it was different seeing large groups of girls living an openly homosexual lifestyle. At a loss for words, I met two of the state's best basketball teams from Memphis, Tennessee. Majority of them were very masculine. Once again I had a flash back of what I previewed in middle school. They were sagging their shorts, wearing high socks, pony tails or braids. I thought to myself, I have a girlfriend back home, so I have to get as close as I can to knowing them and learning their ways without them actually knowing I was in a relationship. Majority of the girls I hung with at this camp saw me as the "church girl" At night I would read my bible, and during worship service I actually worshiped. Though that was authentic, it was also my cover-up at the same time. I wanted to hide my feelings for females as much as possible. Even though these were people that I would more than likely never see again once the camp ended. The very last day of the camp Courtney broke up with me. I pleaded with her over the phone while crying stating that I needed her and how I loved her. After she let me go with no initial reason I figured I was done being gay, I never experienced that type of heart break before. The feeling of reality setting in that the person that you thought that you were in love with drops you as if you really never meant anything to them hurts. In disguise that was an answered prayer from God to help me transition out of the lifestyle I didn't want to partake in from the beginning.

5

Torment, Rejection & Exposure

My dating experiences didn't last so long with guys. It seemed as if the ones I actually liked played games, and most of the guys that showed interest in me couldn't keep my attention. Soon enough my dating experiences with females became some kind of chain reaction, like a domino effect. From that one dating experience with Courtney I had the ability to manipulate female minds, intentional and unintentional. I took advantage of their emotions to get what I wanted, which was keeping them around as long as I could. I treated them the way that Courtney treated me, without realizing that manipulation is a form of witch craft. The type of heart I had would ultimately get me in trouble with God down the line. Tay would become the first girl that I would manipulate unknowingly.

We met during track practice so it was easier for us to get closer which led me to ask for her number. I already knew the intentions I had to pursue her so my approach had to be slick without her picking up on what I was doing. I was so excited to converse with her once I made it home, I walked outside so no one in my house would hear our conversation. Anxiously waiting to hear her voice as the phone rang I walked along the street thinking of what all I would say. I had this strong urge to get to know her and strangely I wanted to see where she was in God, which led to me asking if she'd ever dated a girl before. She proceeded to say she hadn't done so, but wouldn't mind. From that moment on, I knew that I could have her.

As we got closer and feelings began to grow. Most of our time was spent between class and track practices. Track meets would be the only place we could spend all day together, which I loved. I finally had my first girlfriend who was close to my age, and it felt good to experience this with someone who would receive my love, show me love and not shut me out like Courtney previously did. But the more the pressure begin to weigh down on me from the conviction of the Holy Spirit, the devil attacking me, and the love I wanted to provide for Tay, it was all too much for me to handle.

The devil has this tactic that he uses frequently manipulating you into believing that what you're doing is ok and then tries to kill you. Simple as that no sugar coating it. The devil knows God's word he's been here since the beginning watching it unfold so the quicker he can trap and deceive you the faster he can take you out of this world. I began to question God, which would turn into a slight dislike for him. *James 2:19 you believe that God is one; you do well even demons also believe that and shudder.*

The more I strayed from God, the more I turned that energy I once gave to God on to Tay, giving her love and attention that I knew she desired and deserved. God faded into the background and the devil became more visible literally. The same spirit that had been standing in the shadows for years was back. The only difference this time I actually feared what I saw. I was new to gravitating to this lifestyle while trying to live for God and on top of experiencing the devil fighting me each night. The spirit of homosexuality was weighing down on me, God gave me the signs, but I ignored them. The first was torment, second rejection, and last was exposure.

Every night as I fell asleep, my body would rise off the bed and fall back down on the mattress. I couldn't make out as to why I was such a big target. When the devil knows that God has placed a calling on your life his job is do everything in his power to terminate that plan. So of course he had to attack me when I'm most vulnerable and that was in my sleep.

One night I asked my mom if Tay and one of our close friends could spend the night. I was so shocked at her positive response being yes.

The night went by and we were getting tired from our constant giggles and jokes, so I told Tay she could sleep in my bed, and that I would lay on the floor. In the middle of the night, I decided that I would get into the bed with her. Just the comfort of me holding her and lying next to her brought me more joy than anything. I just had a great desire to give out my love to those that were broken. I could pretty much sense when a person is gravitating towards someone to love them. I wanted to give out what I wanted in return which was love and emotion.

As I got into the twin size bed with her, I began to kiss her. I had never gotten to do this with anyone. I was just so excited to show someone the love that they deserved. The desire I had to do things I never experienced before began to form an imagination of *what if* in my mind. *What if I take this further?* However, the rejection from her that night didn't allow us do anything further than kiss, and I respected that. That would be the second warning from God.

Around three or four that morning I saw and heard my mom open my bedroom door. I was still in the bed with Tay under the covers. This lifestyle was something my mom and I had not discussed, though I'm sure she had an idea. She would not let this issue slide by and eventually it was brought it up the next day.

"Why were y'all in bed together?"
My mom asked in a slightly rude voice.

Of course I wasn't going to tell her I was in the bed with her because she's my girlfriend. Oh no! That's too easy. Only God remembers my response to the question. I probably just shrugged my shoulders and lied as usual.

As the months went on, sign number three, exposure, was approaching. Tay and I had the same friends and they all knew about us. By this time, I had told my own close friends about how I felt I was going through a phase so they were all so understanding. I would always ask myself countless nights alone, okay why are they still my friends knowing that I like girls. I would pray to God that they didn't think I looked at them in that way because I definitely wasn't attracted to them. They were all boy crazy. I enjoyed hearing their stories at sleep over's or during random girl talks after their dance rehearsals.

One night we all slept over at our friend Kayla's house, and I remember telling them about the feelings that I was experiencing. I told them how I most definitely knew it was a phase. What was good enough for me at the time, was that I was never too comfortable in feminine clothes, so the fact that guys would still approach me, somewhat gave me a slight approval. As we ended the conversation about the new lifestyle I was pursuing, they said *"Foster, its okay! We still love you!"* This alone gave me validation and led me to believe that it was okay for me to experiment and figure out who I was and who I wanted to be with. From then on I didn't feel as trapped since more people actually knew because it came out of my mouth. First my best friend Patti, Tay's group of friends and now my friends.

I recall my mom dropping me off at a friend's house one weekend and they were planning on going to the American Legion, where parties would happen every other Saturday or Sunday. As I got out the car, I'm sure I had on some basketball shorts, and they were in agreement *"Nuh uh! We about to find you something to wear."* My mom laughed as we said our goodbyes. It was almost as if I was their life-size Barbie doll. We went into one of the bedrooms, and they squeezed me into some mini blue jean shorts, a white tank, and a green fitted shirt and proceeding in doing my hair. I felt somewhat confident, but not comfortable in the clothes I had on, because I loved to be covered. I didn't really care for the attention.

Spiritually God covered me so well, and I never understood why. While seeing many stay in the closet and hide in their pain of wanting to come out, I was nearly out at this point in my life, without publicly announcing so. I figured everyone already knows, so if they want to hear it come from my mouth they can ask me. God never allowed for my church family to bash me, though messages my pastor preached about the gay lifestyle that had me cringe in my seat and feel convicted and uncomfortable. I still was loving my life though pain slowly followed me because of my indecisiveness with being with Tay seriously.

We would finally come to an end, She was tired of the constant break up's and arguments. I couldn't give her all of me because that part of me belonged to God. He owned me and was not putting me up for sale to the devil. All of this would soon fade away, and I went back to dating guys, because it was almost as if God became that annoying sibling that keeps asking you to take them to the store. I decided to give in and try to live a straight lifestyle without actually killing that demon notice I said try. I evicted it from the home it once lived in so I could move my "straight" emotions in to cover up the pain I had yet to deal with. You have to deal with strongholds not push them off to the side. That was the number one mistake I had begun to make starting with Courtney. I would think that I could get rid of my homosexual emotions by talking to the opposite sex, without facing those feelings head on. First problem I had was not knowing anyone who had come out of that life style at that particular time. I figured I could brush the feelings away as long as I could. You must expose the devil for who he is. Whatever your facing you can't brush it off and not expect to comeback. You will give in because you haven't dealt with it.

Around this time I had stopped attending church for about eight months, so I felt out of order like a broken vending machine. Typically, those machines are stocked with your favorite snacks, candy, chips, cookies etc., which would be considered junk. In order to receive this junk, you have to deposit a certain amount of money for it to dispense. I had no opportunity for God to deposit into my life so I could empty out my junk. I was a fully stocked vending machine, full of junk that was out of order, until I was repaired.

My mom and I were arguing more around this time and her personality and my attitude would constantly clash. Through my eyes it seemed as though she never saw my view on things growing up. I really faced a trying time in my life where I didn't want to live anymore so I decided running away would be my best outlet. I put no thought into actually running away. If anything I was just running away from my problems. My emotions, the lifestyle I was trying to get away from something that was inside of me. It's impossible to run away from yourself. I drove myself crazy, my mind was racing and I felt so trapped in the lifestyle that I wasn't sure what my next step would be. Many feel if they come out from behind closed doors that it will make them feel better. I came to learn that the more I opened and closed that door that it brought me more confusion. I needed a way to cope. I needed a way to close the door and never go back but I wanted to leave everything that came with the lifestyle behind that closed door. Lying, pain, deceit, unwanted emotions, outward appearance, addictions, manipulation and so forth I wanted to lock all of those remaining strongholds away forever.

I packed a backpack with tennis shoes and Ralph Lauren Polo's and took off walking late that evening. I wasn't thinking at all. I recall a guy classmate of mine driving the opposite way back towards my house, he asked me if I needed a ride. I told him no thank you and kept walking, I remember him telling me to be careful. God's grace was very sufficient, and I had more favor over my life than I could imagine. I could've easily been raped, ran over, kidnapped, killed or even thrown in the canal to drown.

Even when we are so distant from God and we treat him as if he doesn't exist, his love for us will never change. That night people could've said rest in peace Foster but God was ultimately saying rest in my peace. He wanted me to trust him, but I put all of my trust into something I hadn't even put thought into. Ironically enough, God was giving me subliminal messages to go back home. I called someone that I was involved with to pick me up and they came in no time, but soon told me I would have to figure out where I'm going to go because they were getting ready to go out to a party I remember saying "I really don't care what yall do with me; I'll even sit in the car." So they brought me to my church, and all I could do was cry. That night I ended up back at home. My mom never even knew I was gone and that night I learned running away doesn't mean the problem disappears.

6

Out of Order

A few years passed by, I had talked to a number of girls, but I focused on relationships that involved guys. Senior year approaches and I finally decided to give Jake a chance. We talked on and off since our ninth grade year, but I just couldn't take him seriously. I wanted to take the easy way out and just become a play sister of his. The relationship was very short lived so we just remained friends. Slowly but surely I began falling back into my old lifestyle. The same pattern I'd followed for years had developed. If the relationships I had with the guys I dated didn't meet the standards I required, or if I didn't have interest, I would end up dating a female. When the relationships with females wouldn't work because of the conviction from God I would end up back dating a guy. Just a recurring cycle that felt never ending.

After breaking it off with Jake I prayed and asked God to send me someone I could be with that I could love. Our lack of patience with God can mess up what he's setting up for us. We confuse what we believe is a blessing from God with what is truly a gift from hell. You must be careful what you pray for. God did not answer that prayer, the devil heard and stepped in.

Meeting this new girl Kylie would finally feel as though my prayers were answered and I finally got what I wanted. However once I received it, it wasn't what I really needed in my life. I was so certain that I got the love of my life, and no one could stop us. We met on Facebook in April 2010.

Seeing her online, I remember her flirting with someone whom I didn't really care for. So the jealous side of me had to step in just to take her mind off the person and focus her attention on me. Manipulation at its finest was back once again. Why? Because that was another trait/stronghold that I'd yet to let it go.

On top of battling this stronghold of homosexuality, the house we were living in at this particular time, the same familiar spirit from my childhood had followed me. I knew the devil wanted to take me out. I would have a hard time getting up, I couldn't open my eyes, and my body was stuck as if I was a statue. When I was awake my body felt dead. After this happened with Tay, you would think I got the point. The main reason I repeatedly broke up with each girl was because I felt like God was warning me. The conviction alone that I experienced should've warned me enough. One night in particular, as I was being held down, God allowed for me to see myself running through my room while it was on fire. It was as if an explosion had taken place that very night in my room, but I was running in slow motion. I felt that I could never reach the bedroom door to escape. It represented me losing my soul and spending eternity in Hell. That was one of the many wakeup calls that God personally delivered to me.

For every temptation God makes a way of escape, but ultimately during this period in my life I never understood why God let favor fall over my life the way he did. At the time I didn't know anyone who was living for God but living this unaccepted lifestyle at the same time. He knew what plans he had for me in the future. Jeremiah 29:11 states, "For I know the thoughts that I think towards you, thoughts of peace and not of evil to give you an expected end." As I straddled this fence for years, I came to terms that God would just have to love me for me and accept the fact that I really wanted to pursue this relationship with Kylie. Mistake number one, doing things without consulting God. Seek ye first the kingdom of God and all these thing will be added unto you. I decided to do things on my own this go round.

That's like telling your mom in the African American home that you'll wash the dishes when you feel like it. I know if I ever said that my mom would slap the taste out of my mouth. God has a funny way of punishing us, it starts off graceful but later he allows for things to happen. At least 1-2 times a week, the demonic spirits would hold me down. I would often say "THE BLOOD OF JESUS!" repeatedly in my mind to come up. This was sign number one of the many signs that I would soon ignore in this new found relationship.

Being with Kylie felt like a new life for me. I fell for her in a literal matter of minutes. My own personal conviction from God always assured me that dating the same sex was wrong. I took God's mercy for granted just because he always showed me visions of helping others, so I just knew deep down inside he would never let anything happen to me. Some of the thoughts I had were so irrational. I thought that God would never kill me, because he needed me. *"Who else is God going to use? No one is Foster."* I was cocky with my choice of words, and with the thoughts I often had towards God. I felt high and mighty because of the pedestal I was placed on by people, so I ran with it.

I took advantage of my relationship with God. I felt that because I had a relationship and a connection with him that he would give me time to play around and come back when I was ready. The warning signs started early, and of course I ignored them so I could spend all my time with Kylie. I came across her through social media and started scrolling through her pictures, and began flirting with her right away.

She became my initial charge. Anytime I needed love, felt low, or needed attention she would charge me up, I never died. My flesh was livelier than it ever was. I definitely had life backwards. The fact that I wasn't trying to kill my flesh was my free ticket to Hell, no need to pay for one. This wasn't even because I was Foster, that's just going by God's word, but a trip to Hell is an extended summer vacation with no return hotter than the Sahara Desert. No need for me to pack because my flesh was packing enough. I had a backpack busting through the zippers packed with pride, deceit, anger, lust, and on top of that, I was indulging in a gay lifestyle that God did not approve of.

The bible is very clear of this lifestyle. Starting in the book of Genesis 2:24, it clearly describes that a man should leave his parents to be with his wife. Throughout the Bible it makes it clear that marriage is made for a man and a woman. Many like to argue with the old testament in the bible stating that we are no longer under the law but we are now under grace. But God's word does not change. In the New Testament 1 Corinthians 6:9 states that wrongdoers will not inherit the kingdom of God, neither the sexually immoral nor idolaters nor adulators nor men who have sex with men.

Aside from my new acquaintance, there was a lot going on in my life. My graduation party was coming up the following week, along with prom. I didn't have a job my senior year I was an entrepreneur since freshman year, making t-shirts and selling snacks out of my locker.

A friend of mine was selling her homecoming dress, so we headed over to the north side of Beaumont and bought the dress for $100; I was so grateful. Kylie and I would make jokes about me wearing a suit and her being my date, but I knew that wouldn't happen. The night of prom my date and I arrived at Cheddars, I was too anxious to order any type of heavy food from the thought of seeing Kylie afterwards.

She and some of her friends purchased a hotel room for that night and man I envied them. I thought, dang! This is my prom night and I don't even have a room, but my mama was not going for that nor paying for it. So envious or not, a hotel room was not up for discussion. We finally arrived to Lamar University pulled up to the Setzer Center where prom was held.

There was an instant reaction that came from everyone seeing me dressed up. I usually just dressed tomboyish when I went to school. Despite the nice compliments and the good vibes from my friends and associates I wasn't enjoying myself at all. It was more of a, "let's take pictures sit down and look cute type of event" and no one was dancing.

All of a sudden as I looked up one of my friends began walking towards me and my jaw immediately dropped. As if my night couldn't get any worse, she had on my dress! A few minutes went by and we joked about it and even took pictures together, so I couldn't stay upset too long. All the while my date still made me feel awesome. By the time they announced the prom king and queen, people began to exit.

As we left prom my date asked, *"What do you want to do?"* I responded rudely *"Just take me home "Well, let's at least ride around or do something, "* he said trying to make the night better and make me feel better.

This was my first boyfriend and he was such a sweetheart and was only trying to make my night go a little better but I quickly declined the offer. He took me home and I instantly put on some basketball shorts, Nike slippers, and headed over to the Holiday Inn to see my crush. I was so excited because seeing her would be the highlight of my night. We had only known each for maybe a week or so, but there was something different about her. When I arrived I didn't know any of the people there, but I'm sure they knew of me. There was about six of us, girls and guys. I walked in and Kylie and I sat on the floor texting each other. The lights were off and everyone was watching TV. I made the attempt of asking for a kiss through a text message. I was so nervous.

As the lights from our phones went off we went in for our first kiss. In that moment I just knew I was in love. All the emotions rushed to my heart I literally felt all the same emotions I once had for Courtney, Tay and every other girl I had a short interaction with, but this was above all of the girls. I guess you could consider this love at first kiss. The next day was my graduation party. I wore red vans, ripped white jeans and a custom hand painted shirt that I made. It was a nice turn out, but I was waiting on that one person to come. After anxiously waiting, Kylie finally showed up with a card in hand. I was so glad she showed up. Although everyone loves presents, I was always the person that wanted love as a gift. I always wanted something that would stick and last. The front of the card was suede black with neon colors and it read, "Way to go, Graduate!"

As I opened it I saw that she had drawn "Foster girl..." written on the left side. On the right side, the already printed words were short and simple, "So proud of you." Beneath it in big bold letters written in sharpie, it said, "Congratulations, Love Ky "As I looked to the bottom of the card, she wrote "wish I would've met you earlier" and at that very moment I knew we were on the same page. My feelings escalated as my conviction raced. I thought back on walking her to class for the first time in the last final week of my days as a senior. She was so happy, little did she know that her smile wouldn't last for long.

In May of 2010, I asked her to be my girlfriend. She would always show me immense amounts of love when I felt like I wasn't getting any at home. My mom and I both had soft hearts but when it came down to arguments, we held our ground. I had a smart mouth and I would disrespect her authority. If she let me use her car at times, I would purposely stay out later than she said. If she said do something, I typically didn't do it. Usually if a parent is yelling at the child, the child may mumble under their breath or say one thing, but I began to rebel and I began to yell back at her. We would mainly argue about my attitude, but I was just done and I had let the devil in my life by this point.

I felt as though I had to search for happiness and that's why I stayed with Kylie I just wanted to love and be loved.

7

Graduated and Promoted to Sin

June 5, 2010 was graduation day, and I was super excited. I was so ready to leave Central High School and get away from everyone so I could live the way I wanted without being under a microscope. Kylie wanted to hold up a sign for me at graduation, so I went over to her house that morning, greeted her family, and headed to her room. I started drawing the sign right away. It wasn't anything special, just something quick because I had to go.

I graduated at the Montage Center, and all of our family, friends, and loved ones were there in support of our class of more than 500 graduates. I graduated Cum Laude and was selected to lead the prayer at the beginning of the ceremony as class Vice President. This would be the day I could leave behind the titles I held as president of several organizations, and the pedestal I was placed on living for God would be thrown out of the window. I couldn't live a double life anymore. I was ready to leave church and finally live the way I wanted.

The following night was project graduation. This night was always a fun night for seniors and one of the last times we would be together. The food was in abundance along with candy, snacks, and activities. We would be locked in the girl's gym until 6am.

My ex-boyfriend Jake received a full ride football scholarship to one of the best universities in the country. That night I went out to his car and cried saying I would miss him, though I was still finding myself and I had dated multiple guys he was someone that I finally connected with without losing interest. Everyone knows that when you go off to college the chances of you staying with someone you dated in high school was slim. Once our relationship fell off so I figured that I would finally be done with guys.

That following Monday was full speed ahead for me. I didn't get a summer break because it was time for me to begin college. I attended Lamar University in a summer program for incoming freshman. Class was super early in the morning so I would go to class with a du-rag fitted cap and basketball shorts. I was still covering my identity by justifying the masculine clothes with what I thought was logical explanations. *Oh, I'm just being comfortable since it's so early in the morning.* I continued to lie to everyone, including myself beginning to believe my own lies. My true intentions were to continue dressing the way I've already chosen. While in class although I should have focused, my mind remained on Kylie. She and I would text all day expressing to her how I missed her and couldn't wait to come see her. It was summer so that meant all my time would be dedicated to her. Sometimes if I had to study I'd pick her up and head back on campus and we would stay in the library for hours. I would take her out to eat, or we would stop at fast food places, I definitely had her spoiled. I was living the life I was once longed for, I finally got to show compassion to someone and not have to hide it.

On one particular day we went to Wal-Mart and we began to talk as if we were expecting a baby. We looked at clothes and baby carriages, but not to actually purchase, just to pretend as if we were. We laughed, joked around, and did goofy things like putting on undersized jackets and acting like little kids. The little things that I loved to do made her laugh, and her smile made me happy. By this point, I could care less how God felt. God was allowing me to have my fun, or so I thought. We began to date and we were always out going places, I barely knew her, but I was determined to get to know her. One night on our first date we went out to eat and she let me borrow one of her shirt. I wore some cargos, and I brought my purse, but I made her wear it so I could carry my stuff in int. At this point in my life I was really confused on who or what I wanted to be.

This happiness however, was only brief. Not even a few months into our relationship, I was telling her we had to break up because it wasn't right. Yes, God will let you have your fun or so you may think, but remember he has a plan and a will for the way he wants you to live. Yes, we have free will to live the way we want; however, it comes with consequences. This life really doesn't belong to us it belongs to God, our creator. I know that may not sound believable or make sense, but while we're here on Earth there will be plenty of things we will never understand.

I am positive that Kylie didn't really understand what I said. She knew me as this person who knew God's word, but I was going against what I had acknowledged as evil in his eyes. Better known as a hypocrite. Even so, I fell hard for her, so it wasn't that easy letting Kylie go. Going through the summer sessions at Lamar University, I was beyond confused. I wanted to be openly gay, but battled the thought of what people would actually think about me. I didn't realize that my outward appearance had already spoken for me. I slowly fell into a deep depression. I loved my girlfriend at the time, but couldn't be with her like I wanted to because of the conviction. It was so heavy it outweighed every decision I wanted to make.

Night after night, I would wake up having panic attacks, or with my heart racing, making it hard for me to fall back asleep. Not to mention that I would always see the spirit of death standing in my doorway. I felt as if I was being held down in my sleep by the devil himself.

Imagine seeing your friend asleep on their bed, but all of a sudden you see their spirit get out of the bed screaming for God to help them while their body is still laying there. I went through this for countless nights. Once I finally fell back asleep, I would feel my body being raised off the bed and fall back onto the mattress all throughout the night. There was nothing I could do about it because I had strayed so far away from God. It's almost as if my prayers were being blocked out by my own disobedience. I wasn't attending church I felt no need to go anymore because I was trying to become my own person, and I really wanted to live this life on my own without the correction of God.

The fall semester started and I had at least seven breakups with Kylie. I decided we should only be friends and just date. I thought that if I just dated her, it wouldn't count in Heaven as being gay. I know it sounds crazy, and I don't know what I was thinking. Mentally, it was a trick of the enemy to keep me bound. The devil has a funny way of capturing us. What's weird is we actually fall into his schemes. The months passed by and the relationship became rocky. She was fed up with me breaking up with her, but still showing her an abundance of attention. I was as in love with her as she was with me, so it really wasn't as easy to end things as I anticipated. I honestly didn't want it to end.

There was actually a break into our relationship where I was approached by several studs (a female who dresses like a man). The devil was trying an alternative route, I guess he figured I was going to end it with Kylie for good, so he had to target me with someone who looked like someone I would now try to approach which would be a male. One of the studs I conversed with I slowly but surely begin to fall for her though the conversation was good at the time the love I had for Kylie outweighed any love that was thrown my way including God's because I shut out the outsiders. Though we were not together, I felt like I was cheating on her.

Some nights on my way out of Kylie's house I would just hold her and cry because I hated going home. I wanted to spend all my time with her. She became everything I focused my energy on since my mom and I were very distant during this time. Unfortunately, Kylie was tired of the constant heart ache and putting on a front for people.

At the beginning of our relationship, she wanted us to go public on Facebook by changing our relationship statuses. Though in reality everyone knew, it's different once you go to social media with your personal life. I explained that I wasn't ready for that yet. We were already posting pictures and videos along with sentimental statuses about each other. The entire period was a struggle. While in love, I was also slowly getting ready to collide with depression.

There was always that certain percentage of me that wanted to live right no matter how much my flesh outweighed God. By the time 2011 rolled in I was on my way to destruction. I had pushed her too far with my indecisiveness; she would not take me back. I begged all her friends to help me out. "Please talk to her for me I need her," I would say. I talked to all her best friends for help and asked for relationship advice. I tried to get answers that I already knew. I searched for validation to approve my sins. I wanted to feel secure and trick myself into thinking that my feelings for her were okay. In actuality, God was showing me the repetitive signs visible in the previous relationships. They all ended the same way. That awakening pierced my convicted soul.

I had become so confused in this lifestyle that I felt lost and trapped. I was beginning to be attracted to girls who looked like me, studs. Anytime Kylie and I would stop talking throughout the relationship, I found myself attracted to several girls who resembled a male. I figured since I didn't like guys I might as well have the artificial version a girl who looked like a guy which was even better for me. However, I couldn't stay away from Kylie. My love for her was a stronghold in itself.

Within a year's time I had gotten into two wrecks in my mom's Honda Civic. In one accident, I had just picked Kylie up and not even three minutes down the road we got hit. My mom's car spun into a parking lot. Ky' mom rushed to us and followed me home to make sure I was okay. The car suffered extensive damage.

Kylie and I were always together and my mom realized a change in clothing and the way I act. We had yet to discuss my sexual preference, except for one particular time. She asked, *"Christian are you gay?"* I laughed and said, *"No, mama, and if I was, I wouldn't tell you."* She pressed again, *"Would you tell me if you were?"*

Prior to that accident, I left my phone sitting down somewhere and I'd just changed my screensaver to a picture of Kylie. Funny how the Holy Spirit still protects us even in our mess, something told me to go and grab my phone, but I thought nothing of it.

"What is this?" she said. I couldn't say anything. Kylie was my phone's screensaver.

Many of you may not understand the lifestyle. Most people wonder as to why you would date a female whom looks like a male when you could just date one. It's simple and that is attraction. You may know someone who is living in the homosexual lifestyle and you feel they need one encounter with the opposite sex to become un-attracted from the same sex. That's not how it works your job isn't to convert, your job is to guide and show the love of God in their transition. You absolutely cannot force someone to like or love anyone.

I can recall inviting her to church, because the side of me that loved God wanted to save her soul. But how could someone lost save someone else's soul? Truly I needed someone to save me.

God presented ways of escape for my temptations, but I never took them. I always chose a shortcut instead of taking the highway that God laid out for me. I took the back streets, ones with so many stop signs and obstructions that my path remained compromised. My estimated time of arrival moved further and further away from me.

The delays in my journey were all my fault, results of my choices: first, Courtney, Tay and now Kylie. I just didn't understand why God allowed for all the other gay, bi or curious people, or anyone else in the LGBT community, to go on with their relationships and not have the same repeated problems I was experiencing. He showed me that I was wrong and that he sends the conviction towards everyone before they have a reprobate mind. Warning comes before destruction. Your destruction may not be present here on Earth, but if you were to die at this very moment hell would represent your consequence. So I decided to get back into church and refocus. I was losing myself behind a person who didn't deserve the uncertainty of how I wanted to live life. Kylie didn't deserve to receive the hurt and pain that came along with being with Foster. After we broke up for the last time I fell into a deep depression.

Every night was a constant mental battle for me I cried every night, because I was convinced that she was done with me for good. I tried multiple ways to end my life. I just didn't have the courage to do so because I knew by killing myself it would not actually kill Christian.

When you try to take your life the only thing you take away is your body, the emotions that you show towards people and your presence on Earth. Once you kill your body, your spirit is alive and will bust Hell wide open and will continue to live forever and ever. Think of three things that smell really bad here on Earth. Now combine all those together, the smell will be worse. Think of three insects you can't stand crawling all over you. Now think of three scary movies that you wouldn't dare watch alone, now imagine all those emotions of fear combined with demonic spirts ten times worse torturing you in the dark amongst burning.

That's the ultimate reason I chose to suffer on Earth with depression rather than take my life. Though I tried letting the wheel go while driving over a 100 miles per hour it was always something that drew me back to the thought of my mom. Taking your life is selfish. What about the other people that love and care about you? What about those that would never get closure because you wanted to take away a pain or emotion that could have been temporary if you gave it to God. Even if you are someone who says *Christian I don't have anyone who shows me love this is why I want to take my life*. I encourage you to look beyond people, seek ye first the kingdom of God! Ask God to show you his love and his presence. Maybe you don't even know God or what he stands for or why people worship him. It's simple as picking up a bible start with Genesis, ask God one simple question God if you are real allow for me to stay focus and come out the personal issues that I face. Communication is how you keep a relationship. When you start talking to God your life will change forever your mind will open up in a new way and you will begin to have a different perspective on life and how you should live. It's really all about doing research and finding others that have had encounters with God himself. Those people will be able to show and tell you the different experiences that God has helped them with.

8

I Give Up

A few months had passed by and Kylie had moved on with her life. I was still single, depressed, and only wanting her. I had gotten to a place that I never reached before, a dark place. I had always heard about it but never experienced it until that moment. It felt like my mind was in a jail cell with no lights, but the door is open for you to leave at any time. However, you don't leave because you feel unworthy and numb to anything positive. I had shut out all my high school friends to focus on Kylie, so that when we broke up, I had no friends left.

I wanted to end the darkness. The suicide attempts were constant, mostly occurring while driving in my mom's car. I would be on the freeway and hear a loud voice in my ear. "Just do it!" I knew it wasn't the voice of God because God's voice is calm. The devil's voice is louder like a scream. Well, at least that's how I've always experienced the voice of Satan.

I was finally content after literally begging her to take me back, and I do mean literally. I think she may have blocked me on social media. Her friends finally stopped responding and told me to let her go because she moved on.

In the end, I lucked up because she chose me a few months later. Some would say I was the rebound, but I didn't see it like that. I would say I was just out for the season from a sprained ankle. Once again, it was Chris and Kylie was back in effect. Soon after we made a full year, we ended it for good.

The conviction was too strong and I couldn't handle the relationship any longer, but I made a promise to her as we broke up. A promise that I would end up breaking at least six times. "I promise you are the last girl that I'm going to talk to," I said. How could I make a promise to abstain from something that I had not been delivered from? I figured because I would stop talking to girls, it would make me straight again. I was wrong. That night she was silent on the phone but I heard her tears. I could feel her pain through the phone. The artist Jazmine Sullivan was hot then, so I texted her the complete lyrics to a song while we were on the phone until she fell asleep on me.

"I cannot find somebody else when I know, know that I'm doing wrong, it's so hard, hard to let go. I done went through just about two bags of tissues baby and you looking at me like you ain't the issue baby and though I tried to leave I can't stop missing you baby and I keep coming I keep coming back. I keep going in circles, circles, round and round the way I'm doing you so wrong you just keep holding me down, I feel so stupid, so foolish treating you all this way but what can I say.... I want to go but I keep coming back."

Jazmine Sullivan

Of course, I changed the words to make it out to fit our

situation. Though I knew we would never be together again, I wanted to show her that I genuinely sorry for all that I put her through. But this wouldn't be the last of our communication. I remember praying that night before I fell asleep, asking that God send her someone she could spend her life with, and who would treat her better than I ever did.

9

Broken Promises

Once I decided I would no longer become involved with Kylie, or any girls for that matter I wanted to commit to that promise. Not for myself, not for God but because I was committed to not go back to that lifestyle once and for all. Given my history of constant regret that often led to lasting heartbreak, it seemed worth the risk.

There was a girl, Joy who was a supportive customer and she always put in orders for custom hand painted shirts. This was her senior year, and she wanted to run for homecoming court, so I created flyers for her and many of her supporters purchased shirts to promote her as well. I didn't know that I would soon be performing witch craft once again by manipulating her mind.

What many fail to realize is that the more you're around a certain type of person their spirits can jump on you good or bad.

However, I will not put that blame on Joy, but she did have a history of dating someone prior to me. In a way, you could say her spirit and my residue clashed and formed into something I didn't see coming.

I tell people all the time, when coming out of anything, you have to break communication from those who are involved in what you want to be detached from. I don't care what it is, if the temptation presents itself don't give into it, resist. James 4:7 says to resist the devil and he will flee. Satan wants to see how far he can go with you.

It's the same principle of Eve and the Tree of Life. Contrary to popular belief Eve did not eat that fruit the first time the serpent approached her. The devil likes to push you to your limit he knows what you like. When room is given for the devil to constantly tempt you before you even rebuke him, of course the back door will always be accessible. This is a prime example of why prayer is key, praise is your weapon, and pleading the blood of Jesus a part of your gear for warfare.

I surrounded myself in Joy's presence. She was so loving, especially since I was longing for this. I had shut Kylie out months prior. It was as if she took her heart and locked it up so I could no longer reach it. Eventually, I was picking Joy up from school so we could work on campaign slogans and ideas.

One night we were on the phone, and for the first time, I was getting to know her on a personal level. Who would've thought this outspoken, bubbly girl had endured so much pain? Something clicked in my mind, as if I felt I needed to save her. However, of course the Holy Spirit was convicting me. I hadn't even done anything. That's the power of the Holy Ghost, it will keep you even when you do not want to be kept.

Prior to the phone call, I remember feeling something telling me not to stay on the phone. That night I could have made the decision to either try this deliverance out again, or become stuck in sin for the next three to four years of my life.

We take sin, grace and mercy all for granted. Sin is nothing to try out, take for a test run, sample, buy and return with a receipt. I took my salvation and relationship with God for granted because I figured since were so close I can do what I want and come back when I'm ready. Somewhat similar to what I was doing with girls. God gives us grace, so if we do something wrong we essentially get a free pass to start over.

Romans 1:19 says everything you need to know about God has been made plain and clear in his word. Romains 1:20 says he gives you everything you need to know, so you have no excuse to say you never knew it was in the word.

Warning comes before destruction and that's where I was headed. My warning came through conviction directly from God. Romans 1:21-23 talks about people who began to worship other idols, so in Romans 1:24 God told them if they wanted to worship the things of the world and flesh, he'll give them over to the sinful and shameful desires of their hearts since they wanted to disobey his word.

This is when you begin to believe that a lie is really truth. In Romans 1:25, God states that they began to worship and praise other things and because of this, in Romans 1:26 God gave them over to shameful lusts. Even their women changed the natural lust into that which is against nature. This meaning natural sexual desires that men and women would have would now become unnatural sexual relations women with women.

Romans 1:27 men also abandoned natural relations with women and were inflamed with lust for one another. Romans 1:28 states they did not want to acknowledge God or retain the thought of God. He played their game and gave them a reprobate mind. Let me come down your row. Homosexuality is not your thing you say? Okay, Romans 1:29-31 says wickedness, evil, greed, depravity, envy, murder, fighting, lying, deceit, gossiping, slanders, backstabbers, haters of God, arrogant boasters, disobeying parents. The bible goes into detail about each everything that we should and should not do, but yet we make excuses daily for why we can continue to sin purposely.

Romans 1:32 goes on to say that you know what you're doing and will surely be put to death if you continue, and not only just you, but if anyone who condones those who do such things. A lot of times when we know we're doing something wrong, we tend to ask God to send us a sign. We want validation from God for what we are doing. The number one example we like to run to is "God loves me." Yes, he loves you, but he hates sin. That's why I broke down Romans 1:19-32. God's word is forever the same.

The church loves to target homosexuality. Not all churches, I've never experienced that. However, social media shows how mean and hateful the church can be, which makes me, as a loving Christian, look like a stereotype of those who treat certain groups a certain way. Someone once said, "The black church will accept someone who killed someone, and allow for them to apologize, over someone who walks in the church just dressed like the opposite sex." I would like to apologize on behalf of those who have ever done this to you, not just gays, but those who sag, wear tight dresses or don't look the part of someone who's supposed to be in church. I apologize for the pain you may have endured from "church people" Rest assure we're not all the same. We have one common interest, and that is Jesus Christ and the love that we have for this man who died for us.

On the flipside, love cannot be used as validation to continue living in sin when God's word has made the opposite clear. My conviction was always my warning and signs.

That night on the phone with Joy, she proceeded to say, "Please don't feel sorry for me" after telling me her personal story. In that moment I felt as though I had to stay. Prior to our conversation I was going to cut off our friendship because I didn't want to feed into the temptation. People say temptation feels good, but I didn't care for it. Temptation for me was like a sample at a grocery store. It could catch my eye, but just because the sample is there doesn't mean I want it. I'd rather have the whole thing than a teaser. That's how I got tricked every time. Temptation was nothing until I got exactly what I wanted. Why have a slice when you can have the whole thing? Why sin half way when you can sin all the way? My response to Joy would be to tell her that I liked her.

I got myself into trouble, and I felt like I had to save everyone from their own hurt, pain, and insecurities replace that with me...Foster. I felt like a dose of me is what each and every person needed, but I was actually the venom. My cure turns into poison every single time.

I can save you with my love and gestures but kill you with your own thoughts. I had the ability to give you depression and a suicidal spirit. I could run your mind into the ground by the time I'm done draining the love out of you that I needed for myself. I'll leave you empty. Though it was never intentional, you really could say it was because I knew what I was getting myself into.

In that very moment of my life, the promise I made to Kylie would be broken. It was all bad timing. Though I liked Joy a tad, I didn't want to really pursue a relationship with her because I didn't feel like I liked her as much as Kylie. But after those words were spoken through the cellphone that night as I sat in the living room in the dark, I knew I had to make a move. I ended up asking her to be my girlfriend knowing that was not the road that I wanted to go down.

Kylie saw Joy and me at the homecoming game together and she knew something was up. Kylie would always know if I was lying, and I didn't even have to say a word.

The next day on my birthday, I had a small get together at the bowling alley with a couple friends and my family. Joy made it her business to show up and come see me before she went to her dance. I really wanted her to stay at the party with me, but I wasn't too upset because that night I knew I would be with her later.

After the dance was over, she called me and we all headed over to Taco Bell, and as we were driving we were ran off the road. One of her friends was speeding and showing off. We went over a curb, just barely a few centimeters from a metal light pole. I gave him a few choice words, but I didn't have much to say because Joy had a mouth on her, and everyone knew she didn't play. The devil was determined to take me out every chance he could. I couldn't imagine calling my mom telling her I had an accident in her car once again.

Either later that night or that week, I remember receiving a call from Kylie. I already knew I was in trouble. I was secretly still in love with her and hiding my feelings, but luckily for me they weren't as strong as they once were. When Kylie called me that night she didn't make small talk. I remember her telling me she was dating someone. God was answering my prayers because I wanted Kylie to be happy with someone who wouldn't keep leaving her multiple times as I had. I vividly remember her telling me she wanted us to work on each other and give it another try, but deep down I knew that wouldn't work. It wasn't because of the conviction; it was due to the simple fact that she rarely opened up to me. Kylie was the type to shut down and I didn't really want to give us a try because of various reasons. She asked me one simple question that night, and I just had to lie. This was someone that I literally spent all day and every day with. She knew me like a book. Kylie knew my every move: when I would say I love you, when I was sad, when I was mad, when I was hungry, when I didn't want to be bothered, and when I was lying. I never knew how she knew that.

She asked, *"Are you dating Joy?"*

I replied, *"Girl no I'm not."*

She was calm and pressed again *"Chris don't, lie to me."*

I repeated, *"Ky I promise, I'm not, that's just my friend I made some Homecoming stuff for her."*

Finally, she said, *"I promise, you better not be lying to me."*

At that moment I knew she still had feelings for me. That night we fell asleep on the phone and that was the end of that.

10

Welcome Back…For how long?

Another year was slowly closing out. Going on two years after graduating high school and I was already in the category of college dropout. An undercover gay Christian just becoming another stereotype and statistic. For some reason, even if my feelings for my girlfriends didn't exceed my feelings for the love I desired, I tended to use gifts as a way to pimp their love. Meaning, my love language at that time would be to give gifts to show someone I loved them. This would be an incentive to keep them around. Though my actions spoke for themselves, my mind was always thinking that I would have to get back to God. My feelings were double sided, not knowing who to love more, God or the person whom I was with.

Time was winding down as another major holiday was approaching. I had already fallen for Joy even more, and got her everything she desired for Christmas. After a few years of miscommunication my dad somehow got into contact with me and explained that he and his wife wanted to get me back into school, but this would require me to move to Houston. They set up a day where I would meet one of the administrators at Texas Southern University. I made it safely and took a tour of the campus and prior to arriving I had already made arrangements with enrolling and setting up my financial aid. I just had to clear two last steps, housing and telling my mom that her only child would be moving to Houston in a month.

We'd finally finished the tour of the campus, and I had fallen in love. I was ready to get started with my new life in another city; it seemed like a second chance at life. My dad took Joy and me out to eat at Luby's. I felt more at ease having her there while out with my estranged father. The Day was winding down and I had to make my way back to Beaumont.

I told my mom about my decision to move, and she was upset, but happy all at the same time. It was bittersweet for her. Christmas was here, and I made sure that it was the best Christmas ever for Joy. I'd remain happy by covering up the fact that I was truly dying to make any girl I was happy with. I sold my soul to purchase happiness for every girl I chose to be with, thinking I was their savior.

In January of 2012, as my step mom and dad were on their way to pick me up for the big move to my new home. One of the hardest days of my life was leaving the people I would miss the most. My family, my girlfriend at the time, and most importantly, my mom. As I stood outside of Joy's house, with her face red and eyes puffy, Joy would make me cry even more. As we said our final goodbyes, I told her that I would see her soon enough.

As those final moments approached for us to depart, I tried to cherish them while saying my final goodbyes. I remember driving off we turned on College Street to hop on the freeway and tears dropped from the edges of my eyelids.

In a sense, I felt as if I was being kidnapped by strangers. Realistically, I didn't know my dad. My only memories were formed from what I was told and the one time I'd seen him five years prior to this day. Then, something in my mind clicked, as I would finally get a chance to live out a movie role in the father/daughter lifestyle. I was very willing to work on the relationship. I was so used to cutting people out of my life by having a low tolerance for not being treated a certain way. This also steamed from an awareness of how I treated my girlfriends. Yes, I treated them perfectly, but it was the way we ended where I knew my karma would come from.

As I settled in their apartment, a few hours from my first day of college, thoughts such as, *what am I doing here?* raced through my mind. Others sounded like, *Okay you're now in my life, but for how long? I'm welcoming you back, but for how long? I'll give him one more chance.*

11

Behind Closed Doors Again

Texas Southern University was now my new home and I loved it. The freedom, making new friends, the atmosphere was all great, but initially you would have to start over. The shift of starting a new school is like starting from scratch.

Going into this new environment, there was a mental decision I had to make. Will I be Holy Foster or Gay Foster? I battled with this tough decision every day when I woke up, because I knew the answer would eventually need to surface. I stayed in Lanier West, an all-girls dorm on campus. My mind began to wander, *would I date my new roommate? Is she going to try to flirt with me? What will she look like? Will people be able to see through my lies?* I went into this new living situation worried about the wrong things. I instantly forgot that I was already in a relationship.

The first time we all gathered in the lobby of Lanier West, I was sitting on one end of a round couch and a group of girls were on the other end. It was the start of the spring semester, so all the girls had already formed a relationship during the fall. *"Hey. We were wondering if you were into girls."* A girl named Tiara asked. I smiled. *"Nah, I just like to dress like this,"* I responded. I felt I had to start off with a lie because I did not want to go through a transition, and no one would believe me if they saw me dressing as a guy one day, and then as a girl another day. Therefore, my reflex was to live this lie, so I justified the way I dressed.

When we lie, we become our lies, and begin to believe our lies. My answer to everyone's question would become a memorized response that I could quickly use without hesitation.

The question was never brought up again. I'd wondered why they asked and later found out a few of them were either lesbians or bisexual. Let's not forget, I was still in a relationship with Joy. Living in another city didn't help our relationship at all. Especially since I began to get directions from God to leave her. *Here we go again.* This chain reaction, I began to notice was forming an ongoing pattern. We ask God for escape routes but always ignore them.

At the end of the day, I would also date certain girls because I wanted to see how far I could go really just to see if they would be with me. I did this knowing I did not want anything long term. It would always backfire on me because I have a soft heart, and I would fall for the girls time after time. Now here comes God, giving me a heads up, *Christian your time is up, cut the relationship off its going nowhere.* Generally, after God began to send me the first or second warning, my relationships would always begin to take a turn for the worst. Joy and I had a deep heart felt conversation about sexuality, past relationships and where we saw the relationship going forward.

The God in me was once again trying to save whomever I was with. It was the number one sign that I knew what I was doing could not last a lifetime. I would always find a way to bring God into our relationship, but it would be a part of the manipulation process. I would mix good and bad to get a positive response. I figured if I could get any girl I was with close enough to God, they would want to leave me without me having to breakup with them.

Joy wasn't up for the back and forth like Kylie put up with. The more I tried to disconnect from her, Robert and I would communicate. I began to develop feelings for him once again as I had done sporadically since we were twelve. He could finally take me seriously and we could focus on becoming something more. I began to express to him that I needed his help to get out of this lifestyle.

Her birthday was coming up, and, of course, we had to do it big. She planned out a full birthday weekend in February. Her friends and I were walking her to class and I looked across the hall, and less than 5 feet away was someone I thought I would never come in contact with again. She was staring at us with an angry look of disbelief. It was Kylie and her friends all she could do was walk away. In that moment I didn't know how to feel. It was awkward but I was somewhat happy to see her. It had been a few months since homecoming that I had got the chance to see her.

We tend to override the Holy Spirit in an effort to do what we want, and we put what God has for us off to the side. I was so focused on making Joy happy that I hurt Kylie to do so. In the process I lost my dad after his return back into my life, and most importantly, I had essentially leased out my soul to the devil. Earlier that day I was trying to find a ride to Beaumont, expecting my Dad to do so something things happened where words were exchanged and once again I said some things I shouldn't have and just like that I let my Dad walk out of my life or should I say I walked out of his life this time.

Later that day, I had to set some things in place for the festivities that were to come so I left the school and went to get my mom from work. Waiting in the parking lot, I received a text from Kylie, and she was going off on me. I called her and immediately started laughing. Joy and Kylie had exchanged a few words and I thought it all was a big joke that they were fighting over me. I'd finally found out how guys felt when girls would fight over them and it felt good. I was still in love with Kylie, so I could not only hear, but also I feel her pain, I could sense every emotion through that phone call. I ignored it by laughing at her.

That night, Joy went to a party, but I wasn't interested in going. When she got back to the hotel, we celebrated. I felt so free like no one could stop my feelings. Not even God. However this would all change once I got back to Houston. It was almost like God began to punish me for all the disobedient acts I did against him.

I wanted to do right by God so I figured that I would give Robert a real shot this time. We had already been communicating, but I wanted to be with him. A couple months passed by, and I remember being on the phone with him saying that I couldn't live this lifestyle anymore. I was getting approached and complimented by many girls on campus, but I couldn't pursue them because it was all so confusing for me. You may wonder why I couldn't date or flirt openly. It's not that I didn't want to I just couldn't. God gives us free will, but I felt like I didn't have that option because I believe in the power of God. I believed he could take me out at any second if I decided to live life that way I wanted.

My heart goes out to each and every person, not just the LGBT community, but any child who is being rejected because of something they're doing that is considered out of the norm. Regardless of how you live your life, criminal, holy, whatever, you should still be loved. You can love the hell out of someone, and I do mean literally love the Hell out of someone. So, with my mom loving me through it all and no one condemning me, why could I never just live my life the way I wanted to? The answer is this life is not mine it's the Lord's. God owns me. He died for me. Therefore, technically, this soul is his, and this body is his.

The book of Corinthians speaks on the temple. "Do you not know and understand that you are the temple of God and that the Spirit of God dwells permanently in you collectively and individually? If anyone destroys the temple of God corrupting it with false doctrine, God will destroy the destroyer; for the temple of God is holy sacred, and that is what you are." We cannot tiptoe around God's word he repeats himself and clearly for us to understand so that we do not miss what we should know.

When I explained to Robert that I would need his help leaving Joy completely, it seemed as if the words registered in his brain, began to scramble, and went straight down to his heart. He completely flipped out. I guess, in his mind it came across as I was cheating on him. Which didn't matter, as we had already broken up we were just talking as friends. He shut me out completely. After that moment, I felt like I could never date a guy again. He was always my go to person when I was tired of girls he become my outlet.

I always felt that if I didn't talk to a girl that meant I had to be straight. But that wasn't the case, and now my go to person would be gone. First Kylie, then my dad, Joy and now Robert. I was shutting people out one after another by living a lifestyle that God did not approve of.

I decided it was time for me to start dating and living for me. Not living for anyone, not even God. You could almost say I had turned my back on God. After Robert shut me out, I figured I would take it slow with girls this time. I was never the dating type just always quick to be in a relationship.

The next girl I met, Lauren, we had begun communicating through Twitter so one day she told me she liked me so I proceeded in asking for her number. She had a complicated situation already going on with her ex-girlfriend. I figured I wouldn't be the super saver foster this time around. I begin to live the life of Foster getting girls. So I begin to live like such but in a respectable manor. Two girls caught my eye which felt new for me. I actually dated this next go round, getting to know them versus actually just being with them.

Graduation parties were coming up for seniors, and I attended a few. I met one last girl who would complete my love triangle; her name was Rae. She seemed so quiet and shy I just had to pursue her. I was invited to her best friend's graduation party, and Rae and I were able to kick it after the party was over. I proceeded to ask her why she was acting as if she didn't know me because she was quiet and shy the entire time I was there. I just wanted to get to know her more.

June was here, and I was attending two graduation ceremonies with one of the girls that I was dating. We enjoyed screaming and cheering for our friend's, even people we didn't know.

After the last ceremony, we were waiting to see one of our friends and, of course, we ran into Rae. She had a look of anger and disbelief on her face. Once she seen me with this new girl she didn't want anything to do with me. I could tell by the look on her face. Even so, I knew she wouldn't give up that easy. That wouldn't be the last of her.

This new girl and I weren't getting serious; we were just dating casually. I was spending more time with her taking her out to eat, buying her gifts, expressing my love to her. We wouldn't last very long because she wasn't interested in going public. By this time, I wasn't experiencing any level of connection with God, no conviction. I was going to church whenever I felt like it. I was living how I thought I should live, thinking that I was ultimately happy.

Summer had officially made its way here and I let all the girls that I were dating go and asked Rae to be my girlfriend. She said yes with no hesitation, and that was the beginning of a meaningful relationship between us.

I had been comparing every girl to the standards of my previous long term relationships. Tay, Kylie and Joy all determined what I would be attracted to. Their aggressiveness, skin tone, the way they carried themselves it all contributed to the bond we shared. I wanted to finally find someone who I wouldn't leave and do right by them when I made this decision. I was finally "out." Beaumont residents knew my sexual preference, but when it came to the people

I interacted with in Houston, I made sure to keep it a secret as long as I could. I even went as far as blocking certain people from social media so they wouldn't see the pictures I posted. For some reason, I was trying to cover something that was no longer considered a secret.

Dating Rae felt so perfect, especially since I made it my business to not up and leave her. She didn't deserve that. Simultaneously, my style of clothing began to make a drastic change. I finally became comfortable in masculine clothing; I even started sagging my pants out in public. However Rae didn't go for that, so I respected her wishes and made sure my pants were a tad higher. Everywhere we went, we took pictures and posted them to Instagram.

For once in my life, I finally felt like God gave me the green light to just do whatever and live how I wanted. Though all of this felt like fate and purpose, there was a piece of me that felt missing. Of course, I now know that a connection with God is what was missing. However, when you're far from God, it may feel that way. Consequently, you begin to fill the voids, to make sure you stay sane and happy when all the time, it is God who should do those things. We take things into our own hands, thinking we got it all under control, just setting up a path for the devil.

After becoming official, Rae and I planned a dinner date. I met her at her best friend's house, took pictures, and then we headed to Cheddar's. It's funny how when you are trying to avoid being seen, that's when you are the most exposed. People come out of the woodwork that you haven't seen in year's people who know your parents, church members, people you don't keep in contact with.

That night everyone that knew Rae just happened to see us together. The first person was sitting across from us at the next table over. One after another, friends and other people began to show up at our table. I thought it was funny, but Rae was a bit frantic posting pictures together on social media its different when you're not behind a screen.

We headed to the movies, and the night ended perfectly. Summer was ending, and my church was preparing to go to Schlitterbahn in New Braunfels, as we did every year. A plan was set in place to attack me. I began to get a tad bit conceited because a lot of "undercover" girls were finally telling me that they were into me. It was too late, however because I was committed to Rae. During this time, I cheated on Rae by getting involved with someone who was showing me attention. It goes to show that you can have it all, but if something catches your eye, it's up to you to have self-control. I was so serious about settling down with Rae that I began to start planning how we could spend the rest of our lives together. I knew her family wasn't going for it, and though my family loved me and cared and supported just about everything I was doing, they would not attend our wedding. I was always making hints at how nice it would be to spend the rest of our lives together. I wanted to plan an engagement at some point in the future.

12

End It All

August 9, 2012 was the day I planned to take my life if God decided to take my mom from Earth. In June, I found out she had stage three breast cancer and had to get surgery to remove it when my mom told me. I responded, "Oh…Okay." It wasn't said in an arrogant way I just didn't want her to see the hurt and pain that came over me. I asked her how long she had known, but I walked out in the middle of her explanation to go into another room. I began to cry and felt like she wanted to leave me because she didn't say those three simple words earlier "I have cancer." In that moment. I became selfish. It was all about me.

Prior to all this taking place, I was still with Rae, and we were pretty serious. This was the first girl who I didn't leave because God told me to. I remained there. I became her everything. I was her escape route. No one else existed in my mind. I wanted us to go further, so I began to ask her how she felt about marrying me. She was somewhat down for it, but: her ex-boyfriend seemed to pop back in the picture suddenly. She decided to give him another chance out of the blue, but I didn't understand because he was gay as well. I remember walking out of Crossroads Bowling Alley on my lunch break and ending it over a text message. I couldn't do it anymore. God allowed for me to have my cake but only eat a slice, he has a funny way of giving you an escape route but I didn't see it that way, I was completely hurt by this girl.

The day my mom had surgery, I told my best friends Mahogany and Sharika what was taking place and that I would love if they came to the hospital that day. I remember going outside with Mahogany so she could cheer me up. As rough as I was looking on the outside I pretended to be happy despite my internal hurting. I ended up texting Rae. I told her that I really wanted her to be there for me even though we weren't together I needed a support system. I got my mom's car and headed to pick her up, speeding as if my mom had only a few seconds to live.

When Rae and I arrived back at the hospital, the doctor called me into the room with my aunt and mom. I walked in and saw my mother laying in the hospital gown as they were preparing her for surgery. I must have cried like a baby while holding her hand, never letting her go. Our final moments together put me in a state of shock, and the reality that I may never see her again set in.

Hours later I was sitting on the stairs, Rae on my left and Mahogany on my right. My eyes were so red. I just kept repeating, "My mama can't die! If she dies, Ima die!" I was angry with God, but I didn't realize he was setting up a plan to get me together.

My mom came out of surgery, but one thing was missing: her

breast. After that, my life changed forever, starting with the way I treated my mom. From here on out, we would become best friends. Who would've thought one surgery would bring a once semi separated mother and daughter together for a lifetime? This was my wake-up call.

It was time for me to get myself together and stop messing with these girls. I started getting more serious with God (for real this time) and tried to spend time alone with myself. However, I didn't know how to be unattached. I had been in a relationship or "talking to" various males and females since 2004, without taking a break. Here it is now almost 2013 and the real truth is, I had a fear of being alone. Sin comes with more and more layers and you only discover them along the way. Now had I just stopped before I had even started the spirit of loneliness wouldn't have carried out this long. That is why it is so key to follow the voice of God and just remain obedient. That stronghold of just being lonely carried out for longer than it should. Just like sin, it's like an unwanted guest that was never invited but the longer you are around it you get to know it more and more. So I had adjusted to being gay instead of telling it to just leave.

One day at TSU, I as with my roommates in our apartment, and as I stood against the wall,

I said, *"I have something to tell yall, but don't look at me crazy."*

They said, *"Okay."*

I continued, *"I've been going through this phase of liking girls, but I'm not even sure if it's a phase"*

They were also raised in the Christian religion, so they understood, but they didn't judge me or show hatred. *"Girl, we already figured that"* they laughed in a comforting way, and at that very moment, I felt a burden lift from my heart. This whole time I was trying to hide these feelings when, in actuality, my feelings were visible through my choice of clothing. Though you can't really judge someone's sexual preference from their closet, I was one confused induvial, and I had gotten to that point of always wearing masculine clothing. They understood, and we began to have bible studies in our apartment together. The devil was mad because he knew they would be praying against the spirit and that stronghold within me.

That's one the devil's tactics, he makes us believe that it is pointless to share how we truly feel with anyone. He allows us to go through life thinking no one is going through similar experiences, able to understand, or even help. It's a trick of the enemy, and you must bind it in the name of Jesus.

You must reveal yourself to someone you can trust, and that's how a domino effect begins. They can pray and intercede for whatever you need, and then doors are opened, and miracles manifest. God places people in a position to help you.

However, even with this burden lifted, I immediately fell into a deep depression. I just wanted someone to love me. I was transitioning in all areas of my life. I was in a sporadic relationship with a guy from my high school. I felt comfortable in the clothes I chose to wear because he approved of my attire. He even bought me my addictions: high socks and snapbacks. However, I had to let him go. I was repeating the same cycle I did with every relationship.

I had no family or friends here that I could really talk to

because I had lied to them about being gay. What would that look like, going to them for help? As I sat in my dorm room for countless days, I contemplated suicide. I was upset with God, and I didn't understand why was I being convicted for my feelings. I didn't understand why could every other gay person could be happy and live their life, but I couldn't. I wanted answers from God but never got them. I believe now that he was showing me I was chosen, and though those people may be happy on the inside, there is a small voice deep down inside that is telling them it's wrong. God was showing me that I had to be the one to stand up and fight it off because he was not going to let me die in sin.

I wanted to jump out of the third story window and end it all. How could someone well-known and so loved get to a place where they felt so lonely, unloved, unwanted? I felt like I was invisible to others and no one could see my pain. However, I wasn't trying to make it known. I wasn't trying to make myself vulnerable. I stayed hidden and didn't seek help. You can't expect people to read your mind, even your body language tell them exactly how you feel and what's bothering you.

That day, I sent my old roommates suicide note in the form of a text, although not as deep or straight-forward. They tried calling me, but I ignored their calls. They decided to come up to my room, by this time we now lived in different buildings.

They ended up calling one of my high school friends that used to attend TSU and told her the situation. Amanda George was her name. She and her mom drove the 72 miles from Beaumont just to come talk me out of ending my life. At that very moment, I knew someone loved me. Who would drive all the way from the comfort of their home to talk to someone, especially a person that loves God? Once they arrived her mom sat at my desk and Amanda sat on the bed with me. I felt as though they just wasted gas and time. My plans were to end my life once they left. An hour passed, and in that one hour they talked to me, shared things they had never shared with anyone. Their words changed my life forever, and I knew I had to get my life right. Maybe you wish someone would show up to rescue you like this. Well I have good news and his name is Jesus he died and came back to life just so that you wouldn't feel the way that you do. If more people were willing to expose themselves more, tell secrets, be there, pray, tell us we're wrong, and love us we wouldn't go through half of what we do, but it all starts with you by seeking help.

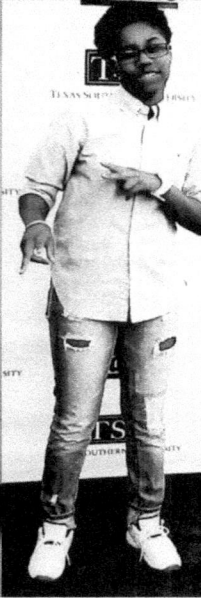

13

A second Chance

I was going through a phase of asking "God, why do I always lose interest with these guys I come in contact with?" It made no sense at all. God even seemed to bless me with respectable guys, the ones who weren't trying to sleep with me.

Once I had the talk with my friend Amanda, I had time to think especially since it was now summer. I felt I needed to just chill out, so I ended up moving in with one of my best friends, Patti.

After a few months, I was visiting a church in Houston near TSU it was an awesome church, it just wasn't for me. Though my spirit was fed, I didn't feel a spiritual connection there.

Sometimes we become so impatient wanting to know what God has for us, and when he is going to come through. However, it's all about perfect timing with God. Things will happen when he feels you're ready. Sometimes, he even waits to see if you're going to reach out for extra help. When I moved to Houston, I expected everything to be handed to me, but God began to humble me. I reached out to Sharika to help me find a new church. This first step of course would rebuild my foundation.

I didn't yet know that 2013 would be the year God gave me a second chance at life. Sharika picked me up one day, and we went church together. Come to find out, she knew the pastor and his wife.

I felt right at home from the first day. Service was even better than I expected. Once church was over. Sharika introduced me to the pastor and his wife. They welcomed us, and I could feel their love. First impressions mean everything, and love was something that did not exist in my life. Just speaking with positivity did something for me. I went home that week anticipating Wednesday night service, and that following Sunday I joined the church I had attended

Months later I was at a Mexican restaurant on Westheimer and drinking heavily, a habit I picked up at TSU. I enjoyed the feeling of being drunk and utilized every opportunity that presented itself. My tolerance was pretty high, so I ordered some enchiladas and Patron. As I headed to the bus stop, a tall brown skinned, older man passed by me. I'm very cautious, so I instantly thought, *Lord Please don't let me have to go into defense mode because I don't have time for it today.*

The man asked " Do you know the Lord"

"Yes, sir" I smiled. "I'm actually listening to a sermon now."

That was my thing. I'd like to get drunk and watch or listen to preaching. At that particular moment, I was listening to one of my favorite preachers, Creflo Dollar.

The Guy spoke and said "If you don't stop doing what you're

doing, God is not going to give you what you want." His words really hit home. I remembered how I had been saving to get a car, but different things were hindering me. I had gotten so frustrated with relying on bus transportation.

Around this time I was seeing Rae again, and began to catch feelings and she had a way of getting to me every time. It was her slight clinginess; loneliness was something I had yet to conquer. The fact that I wanted to marry her one year prior to this didn't help either. I told her we really had to stop messing around with one another but at that time she had my heart.

When choosing a woman to date, appearance was never a factor. At first, it always started out as a challenge; I wanted see if I could get them. It was similar to when guys try to see how quickly they can sleep with a girl.

I was a little different though, I could care less about sleeping with them. I wanted to get inside their mind. I wanted to see how far they'd let me keep them on this invisible string. I continued this game because I knew I wasn't going to be with them forever.

All I wanted in return was simply recognition and love. I wanted so badly to be spoiled and showered with gifts, so I did that for all my exes. It wouldn't be long until I fell for them. Kylie was a prime example. I fell for her less than a week after just seeing if I could pursue her.

I longed to be told I was beautiful. I knew I wasn't ugly per se but it was one insecurity I had deep down. When I looked at myself in the mirror, I felt ugly. I allowed the devil to creep in, and I honestly thought I was more attractive as a guy.

Rae had this thing where she was frequently leaving and coming back. She was the only ex I knew would come back if I called her up.

I had to figure out how to leave this girl alone. It was so hard cutting off someone who actually showed me love, but God stepped in, and I didn't have a choice. Around July I was hired on at my new church and I reached out for help in the midst of my sin. My own personal conviction lead me to seeking out this help. No one forced me as you have read. No one bribed me, not even a tragedy cause me to want to change the lifestyle that I was living. My conviction that I received daily left me longing for something more than what that life had to offer. I was living this alternative lifestyle, and I honestly wanted out. I was fed up of going through the constant cycle of the last seven years. It was a struggle, and I wasn't happy.

God has a funny way of setting up connections God led me to Houston to attend Texas Southern, which led to me finding a church home. He allowed for me to be hired by that same church, and on top of that, my mentor Minister Robin McKnight, would help me come out of this lifestyle. No, it wasn't any type of exorcism, witch craft, intervention going on and we were definitely not trying to "Pray the gay away." I was about to experience raw, and uncut, one on one information from someone who experienced far more than what I went through. My first time actually speaking with her, I walked in the office in my baggy clothes, and she shared her story with me. It seemed impossible for her to even have come out of the lifestyle. Even as I was talking to her, I had doubts about if it would be possible for me.

With God all things are possible so for those who take "Pray the gay way" as a joke. Don't dismiss it so fast. If God can deliver a drug addict, or a cheater or even cure someone from a sickness he can take away those feelings and desires you have for the same sex but only if you want to remove them. I can tell you all day something is wrong but that doesn't matter if you feel you don't need to change.

Months were going by swiftly, and the process was hard. Breaking free of the homosexual lifestyle was very tedious. You must first be willing to submit to the will of God, fast, pray and really read his word for yourself. You must be careful of what you are feeding your spirit in the process. Are you on social media sites where your eyes can get you in trouble? What type of music are you listening to that will influence your thoughts? Romans 12:2 states "Be ye transformed by the renewing of your mind." You must change the way you think to change your lifestyle. How do you think business owners get where they are today? They had to change their state of mind. In a similar way, you need to change the way you think. For example, I would often hear, *once gay, always gay*. I heard it so much that I became those words. It's also important to break all communication from those who will pull you backwards.

I had several conversations with my mentor about feeling the change in my life, but the temptation was coming back. I told her that I had to change the way I dressed I felt that was why I couldn't completely transform into what God would have me to be. She told me that no matter what we are free from, we will always be tried and tempted, that is exactly why James 4:7 tells us to resist the devil. Even in the book of Matthew, after Jesus fasted for 40 days and 40 nights, he was hungry. The devil even told Jesus to jump off a cliff, and kill himself, but Jesus told him, "Satan, get behind thee. Man shall not live by bread alone, but by every word that preceded out of the mouth of God."

Just because you are tempted, it does not mean you have to feed into the temptation and try it. It's one thing to be tempted in front of people you can lie and act as if you don't want whatever your stronghold is. The real test is when you're alone and temptation presents itself. Will you give in or resist? The more I resisted the devil, it seemed as if he fought me even harder. Even so, I had to show him I was serious and didn't want to die like this.

That's the place I had to get to when Rae would come back into my life. I had to delete her number. She had the easiest number in the world to remember, but through God all things are possible. I was able to forget it once I deleted it.

Robin showed me in Deuteronomy 22:5. It states a women must not wear men's clothing, nor a man wear women's clothing, for the lord your God detests anyone who does this. I was in shock because not only was I living in sin, I was walking in sin too. I had no idea that my favorite clothing was hindering me. That is exactly why we must repent for all sins, known and unknown. I was at a place where I would still wear boy's boxer briefs because I'd gotten so comfortable wearing them. My closet was already filled with countless shoes, jerseys, and Ralph Lauren shirts from the little boy's section. I began to pray and ask God to help me live the way he wants me to live God pushes and shakes us out of our comfort zones because he is ready to take us to a new level, a level where we must leave the remnants of sin behind. Though people may try to argue that the Old Testament doesn't have to be followed because we aren't under the old law we are under grace which is true, but grace shouldn't be abused. Different strokes for different folks, no excuses I hated the feelings I had, I didn't want to live in the homosexual lifestyle so therefore the Old Testament applied to my life in the aspect of the type of clothing I was choosing to wear because it affected my life in a way that I didn't care to be a part of.

I finally was able to cut Rae off and things started to fall in my favor. In September 2013, I got my very first apartment, and a few months later, my first car. It was a 2002, all black, two door Pontiac Grand Prix.

Toward the end of 2013, I felt myself actually break free from homosexuality. Although the temptations came, they were not heavy because I was prayed up, and I was mindful of the people I hung with and the things I did in private. I made sure I was staying in God's word whether it was reading or watching.

As 2014 rang in I begin to re-discover some talents I had thrown to the side and given up on. I had my new apartment, my first car, and I was closer to finally ending this life threating homosexual lifestyle, my life goal.

Months would pass by quickly, and my time with my first car would be short lived. The power steering went out twice, transmission went out, over heated, problems with the doors, randomly towed, rim and tire fell off as I was driving and so forth. It had complications because I started dabbling back into the homosexual lifestyle.

God will reward those who seek him diligently, which I was doing. I proved myself worthy for months on end, but let me explain something to you, God will strip your blessing in a matter of moments if you don't get it together.

I finally began to make more friends in Houston, and I met a girl named Monique. My first test was finally here after months of transitioning. I failed…I know your thoughts *now well that means you're still gay right?*

I figured this was my opportunity to see how far I could go with her. I began going over to her house. I was really cool with her family, so I would help with homework assignments, and I noticed she would flirt with me. She would do little things that hinted towards her interest in me. I was thinking, I can still do this. I had always wanted a girl who was saved, but all my ex-girlfriends weren't into church while we were dating.

Be careful what you ask for because God, will send you exactly what you want. Even when it's not necessarily what you need it's just a test. That's exactly what this situation was: a test to see if I would go after the first girl that approached me. I went over to her house every other weekend and helped her with her homework or played basketball with her brothers. Her parents were usually gone, so I had more than enough time to pursue her. One day we went in her room and sat on the floor and I instantly went back into "Foster" mode. My personality was sweet but demanding so I figured this would be easy.

As I leaned in for a kiss, she backed away. *"What the heck!"* I wasn't angry, just cocky. I didn't believe that I could be rejected. I figured I was just rusty, so I leaned in a second time, confident she would kiss me. My lips weren't crusty, and my teeth are straight. Even so, she rejected me once more. *Just give up!* I thought to myself but I tried one last time: I wasn't taking rejection for an answer. I leaned in, and we kissed for about ten seconds before we heard three loud knocks on the door. Thank God her door was locked; it was only her little brothers.

Months passed and my mentor asked me how I was doing, just a routine checkup. I had slipped up. I told her I had done something terrible, and I felt bad about what had transpired. She immediately told me to leave Monique alone. I thought I was strong enough to just be friends with Monique, when, in actuality, she was the charge to my weakness. I was fairly new to my freedom, somewhat like a student of an AA meetings.

Like an alcoholic at a bar, I could go around a group of girls because I wasn't attracted to all women, but I did want Monique. She was such a sweetheart. I was so used to knowing aggressive girlfriends that it felt good to know one girl with a softer approach. It was easier to maintain a relationship with Monique because of our age difference. I had found myself falling for her once again, but I had a chance to save myself before I fell back in too deep. About three months later I decided to get re-involved with Monique. This night, God would interfere in an odd way, but it changed and saved my life.

I was helping her brother with his assignments, but it had gotten late, so her parents would let me stay the night. By this time in our friendship, our feelings were strong for each other, but we knew we couldn't express these feelings openly. The way we were raised wouldn't allow it, she knew about my transition and it just felt wrong.

One thing people don't always understand when dealing with an issue, sometimes one person may consider it a sin, but another person may not. Regardless if a person thinks it is right or wrong, you must go off your own personal conviction. If you don't receive the conviction, or feel God tugging at your heart, simply ask God, so you can be protected in the end. You don't want to go through life thinking the way you were living was God's will when, in actuality, it wasn't.

I hate reliving this moment because I was so sure that I would be killed this night. As I settled onto their couch, Monique and I begin to text, I was growing tired of that, so at one o'clock that morning when I figured everyone was fast asleep, I walked down the hallway into her room without any hesitation.

As soon as I made it inside her room, I began to kiss her and about 3 minutes later, we hear a muffled scream in a deep, masculine voice.

"WHAT YALL IN HERE DOING!" her dad said.

"Oh! We're trying to fix her phone." I lied.

This was the perfect excuse in my thinking because her phone was actually broke. However excuses would not get me out of this one. Come to find out, her dad was standing there and watching us the whole time.

I went back into the living room. It took me forever to fall asleep because, I kid you not, I thought I was going to die! I thought he would come into the living room and end it all for me. Over the next couple of days, I began to dwell on the situation and looked back at my life from a distance. I felt like I had let God and my mentor down.

It's hard to stop communicating with someone you love, but it's even harder if you see them every week you can't avoid them. The next stage of my life depended on sacrificing everything that I once knew in order to get away from the mental closet I had locked myself in. There were more things that transpired in just that small time frame that I cannot discuss, however, God will keep you, even when you think the worst could happen. When God saves you from something, it's best to do everything in your power to not go back. We're always making excuses in this type of lifestyle. We tend to say, "God made me this way." No God did not create you to like the same sex in a sexual way. The times may change, but his word does not, it stays the same. I stress so much that you must find out for yourself. At the end of the day, my testimony can only take you so far in your transition and the process of coming out of the homosexual lifestyle. You have to do the work, but remember you are never alone. God will put people in your path to encourage you along the way.

Monique and I stopped communicating for a few weeks after the incident, and I stepped away from everything to focus heavily on church. However, though I was working there, I'd begun to feel distant from God. That is exactly how the enemy tricks you. He allows for you to believe you are alone and that God is not concerned about you. Before I knew it, I was again involved with Monique, and something I once prayed for was coming to an end. As our relationship continued, my car kept having problems.

When you start operating in flesh and not the will of God everything possible will be thrown at you because of disobedience. One day on my way to work a co-worker and I were about five minutes away from the church, and we were approaching a rail road track. Just as we got to the track, we heard the tire sound as if it was going flat.

As we came to a stop, the car fell to the side of the road. We quickly hopped out and noticed the entire tire had come off the car. In that moment, we laughed, not believing what just happened. The cops pulled up and called a towing company as we began to look for the bolts from the rim. About a month later, the transmission was slowly dying, so I decided to just sell my car and be done with it.

My first car came and went after only seven months. I truly believe that was God's way of getting my attention. I had abused the gift he gave me and was wrongfully using it for my own desires. Just like that, I was stripped of a blessing for disobedience and the way I chose to live my life. It's better to live for God and do things in order. I bet you're thinking I learned my lesson. Well, you're wrong.

One night while I was at home God began to speak to me so clearly, and tears rolled down my face as if I had failed. *Christian, I have brought you out of this lifestyle of homosexuality, I already took it out of your heart, you must be ye transformed by the renewing of your mind. Stop allowing the devil to deceive you, you have passed many test but stop failing the final exam over and over.*

I remember one day at work very clearly. I texted Monique, giving her all my time, but trying to be mindful of not falling back into any traps. The devil will manipulate your mind into thinking, *it's okay talking won't hurt,* but if you are not in a place where your strength is built up, don't do it. This applies to everything. Even if you're strong enough still stay away. Don't put yourself in situations that will get you caught up.

If you have friends who steal, but you want to change, you need a new group of friends. Even once you're strong enough still distance yourself from this group of friends. You don't have to be rude or not converse but always be mindful of where you came from and where you are going.

If you're tired of cheating on your girlfriend or boyfriend, maybe you need to fast from social media for a while. Stop entertaining your flesh, with the heart eyed emoji's, compliments, or messages you receive.

It's up to you to stand up and make a change. How long will you allow yourself to continue the same pattern until you decide enough is enough? Driving yourself to the point of suicide is not when the line should be drawn. When you find yourself making a mistake, call it out for what it is and remove yourself from that type of environment.

As we were texting that day, I was getting ready to pay her a compliment, but I felt a sense of urgency and something tugging on me not to send the message. It was so clear, as if someone was standing there warning me. Warning comes before destruction. Even you reading this you may not agree with some of the things in this book, but take heed and don't take it lightly that you have this book in your possession.

I can't say I was hallucinating because I knew what I heard in the spiritual realm. I followed the path I once knew of disobedience, and I sent the text. I immediately felt something shoot through my brain and my eyes. It wasn't painful, just a weird feeling. As I was about to text her again. It was like something was literally trying to stop me from sending the message. One thing I will never understand is why the Holy Spirit always keeps us and fights on our behalf no matter what.

As I typed each word, I felt like a piece of my soul was leaving my body. As I typed out "I love you" to Monique, I felt God strip my mind and thoughts in an instant. It reminded me of when Scrooge left his body to see how he was truly treating people. I felt like my spirit was dead, and another part of me was getting ready to transition into my personal judgment day. While all of this is taking place, I'm still physically in the church at my desk.

I quickly stopped everything I was doing to gather my thoughts. It was impossible, however because I felt like there was just a blank space of thin air and nothing to grab a hold of.

Just when I thought it couldn't get any worse, my life begin to flash before my eyes like a long, drawn out movie reel. I had waited too long to get right with God. I felt as though he gave me warnings signs early on. He stripped me of things I wanted and needed just so I would spend time with him, worship him and stick to the plan he had for my life.

I felt I had to warn others to make sure they did not go through what I was going through in that very moment. I instantly tried to make a post about dedicating your life to God, so I could post it on Instagram, but for some reason, it wouldn't go through. I tried several apps not understanding why. I felt like my brain was sinking and God wasn't going to allow me to speak his word any longer. How could I blame him? I'd become a hypocrite, preaching and teaching God's word, but not living it in its entirety.

My time had come, and I would spend eternity in Hell. On this particular day, I went into the sanctuary and tried to pray to God, but my words could not form into sentences. I tried speaking in tongues, but that did not work either. God had stripped the presence of the Holy Ghost from me. God wasn't having it. He was showing me that he meant business and that I could no longer play around with him.

I tried to call my mom to give her my final goodbyes and tell her that I loved her, but she didn't answer the phone. I called my grandma and told her what was happening, and she immediately began to pray and assure me that everything would be okay, but I knew it wouldn't be. I knew this time I had messed up. You see prior to this day God came to me in a dream with one final warning, and I ignored it.

I walked into a dark church, and everyone was dressed in all black, no color in sight, as if they were at a funeral. I saw my mom at the back of the sanctuary, but didn't understand why she was crying. I proceeded to ask her what was going on. She didn't respond, and I wasn't visible to her. Eric, my cousin, walks up to us and shouts,

"CHRISTIAN! CHRISTIAN!"

While handing me a note. He was the only person who was able to talk to me. I still didn't have a clear understanding as to what was taking place, so I walked to the front of the sanctuary, and see an imitation of Jesus on a cross. The devil was portraying Jesus, but he was a dwarf. Laughing hysterically the devil said, "You're coming with me, I got you now."

God stripped my mind and allowed for me to die slowly and see my life flash before my eyes. He let me feel part of my spirit leaving my body. It's not a feeling like being drunk or high, it just feels as if a magnetic force is slowly sucking your soul with a vacuum.

That night after work, I quickly called Monique and urgently told her that we could no longer communicate in any form. While expressing this serious issue to her, my brain still felt as it was in a trance even though it was hours later. I felt a slight, indescribable pain. I was about to let her know one last time that I loved her. However, God would not allow for that message to be spoken or typed out. After that night, we stopped communicating. In 2014 she was the last girl I desired to be with.

I'd finally gotten to a place in my life where I was totally sold out for God. For the first time in my life, I had a freedom from a stronghold that I could not explain. The burden was lifted after eight long, depressing years.

That following year of 2015 I decided I'd write my dad a five page letter, going into detail about everything he had missed in my life from the time I was four up until April of the current year. I did not realize how much he had missed of my life until I sat back and read all of the accomplishments, downfalls, and sad moments. He'd missed everything.

Every year he would send a Christmas card to mom and grandma's house. In December of 2014, I was so hurt and in pain, that I opened, the card and ripped it up without reading it. I felt like he could've done something more in my life since I was his first born. Something promoted me to keep the address though, so it remained in a green container that I never went into, almost like a treasure box.

I pulled the address label out of the container typed it into my GPS, and headed to his apartment. I didn't know what to expect, or if he was even still living there. As I saw the location, I thought *Oh my gosh*! He lives about eight minutes from the church. I instantly got disgruntled, but remembered that was not the goal. The goal was to drop the letter off and close that chapter of my life.

April of 2015 I arrived at my dad's doorstep, I did a standard knock and waited for a response. A tall man I didn't recognize answered the door, and I had thought I may have come to the wrong house or forgot how he looked even though it only been three years since I last saw him. *"Is Charles here?"* I asked. *"Hold up,"* the man said as he left the door open. "Charles! Someone is here to see you!" he yelled.

A man with a rounded belly and bald head walked up to the door with a startled look on his face, as if he was about to take his last breath. I walked in and said, *"I just wanted to give you this."* I handed him the letter, and tears instantly fell from his eyes.

While reading he says, *"Yeah, you sure do have a lot of me in you, and some of your mother too."* He laughed. He took me upstairs and gave me a gift he had once tried to give me back in 2012. It was a picture he drawn of President Obama and Michael Jackson in the '80s.

"Do you still draw?" he asked

"I feel like I can't draw any-more; it's been so long I think I lost it," I responded

"Wait one second," he said as he grabbed a black drawing book. He showed me some drawings he'd done in college. *"Whenever you're ready, I want you to start drawing again, draw everyday if you can you're a Foster. Here is my business card with my number on it. Save it and call me anytime I don't care what time of the night it is."*

I had finally closed the chapter of my life of being hurt for so many years. No one ever knew because I was so busy helping everyone else with their problems and hiding my own. I wasn't getting the help I needed. I learned how to numb pain without actually allowing the wound to heal. Now my father and I may speak maybe 2-3 times out of the week and tells me that he loves me every chance he gets and I visit him more often. It feels great to actually have a relationship with someone whom I was once hurt by. If Jesus can forgive us multiple time who are we not to give people a second chance, third, fourth and so on.

14

Locked Door

True deliverance is when you no longer have the desire of what God is not for. True deliverance is renewing your mind in order to transform. True deliverance is breaking all line of communication to those things that are connected to what you once struggled with. True deliverance is when you are willing to ask God to show you what are you doing that's not aligned in his will. True deliverance involves fasting and praying. True deliverance requires sacrifice. You cannot continue to engage in what you used to do in order to be free from whatever your personal battle is. That includes music, listening to the same type of music constantly will slowly plant seeds in your mind. Watching shows that you know you are not strong enough to watch should be replaced with something positive. If you deal with anger you can't continue to watch horror movies and get results. If you deal with pedophilia you can't continue to watch children's movies. If you think about randomly murdering people and you have no clue you can't watch certain shows that plant ideas in your mind. If you have a fighting spirit or get pleasure from gossiping or conflict you should refrain from certain TV Shows and so forth. These are just a few examples that most people don't touch on. You must provide and outlet for yourself. If your struggle includes social media you have to limit your time in viewing the pictures and videos that are not positive to your process. I knew I know longer had the desire for women because the feelings were no longer there, the window of opportunity was not there and even if the opportunity presented itself resisting the devil would cause me to close the window without thought or hesitation. My fear of what God would do to me as result of cause and effect keeps me in line. We take God's grace for granted, we view God as this loving God but he will do what he says he will do. There are consequences for you actions. Through every temptation there is a way of escape, no temptation will overcome you, you have the authority and power to stop it, declare it.

I want my life to be so transparent that no one could ever expose me for something that's hidden. Everything I do is placed out in the open to help the next person. This book is NOT to try and covert you, this is my personal testimony of what God has done for me.

My assignment was to share the truth and expose the devil. If you don't believe what you are doing is wrong in God's eyes, it's simple ask him and wait on a clear response or sign. I asked God if being gay was a sin and as you have read I got my answer, merely off of my feelings alone. It was one of the various signs I have received throughout the years. I chose to be transparent with my life because my life behind closed doors is really your life in front of a mirror.

Words have a funny way of coming to past. I always said by

the time I turn twenty five I would be married. September 24, 2016 that day came to past. I'm now spending the rest of my life with my Shipley donut, my yellow skittle, and my light skinned Allen Iverson, Mr. Kevin Bates. He is all that I need and all that I ever wanted in a man and relationship. It took me some time to figure out that I must accept who God has for me and not try to find who I want for me. God will be give you the desires of your heart, but make sure you consult God first before you decide to choose who you think he has for you.

My desires now line up with the will of God and what he had for me which is now my husband. I don't care to engage into those feelings, activities or lifestyle. I locked that part of my life off a long time ago.

I stand as a representation to now broken generational curses and strongholds. If God did it for me he can do it for you. Speak it into existence it's already done. Do your research for yourself. Don't be fooled there are others out there ready for you to hear their story as well. The enemy doesn't want us to be educated so that he can hold us captive, but I am no longer a slave because her life behind closed doors is no longer open for attack.

Personal Prayer

Thank you God for the opportunity to share my testimony with the individual that has read this book. Bless them like never before. I ask that you forgive us of all our sins, known and unknown. Come into our hearts and save us, help for us to imitate your life as close as possible God. Allow for us to use our daily life to shed light onto others. Allow for our love for you to spread to others instead of judging or condeming. Those that are battling strongholds or generational curses I declare and decree that the curse is broken and ending with the individual reading this prayer now. In the mighty name of Jesus I bind all strongholds that we may be battling in the light and behind closed doors. Father God I ask that you open our spiritual eyes and remove those around us that are not good for us in whatever seasons of our lives that we are in. God please allow for us to build our relationship with you. God I pray a special prayer for those who wants the desire to be more like you also those who may not know how to pray father God send them someone who can show them the way. God I ask that you cover each and every person that is battling with the life of homosexuality even those who may not believe that it has no harm. Allow for them them build a personal relationship with you and conquer all sin. In Jesus Name amen!

NOTES

What is your personal struggle(s)? How Long?

_____

_____

_____

_____

_____

Have you decided to break free from this struggle? Why?

_____

_____

_____

_____

What are some of the things you could do or let go in order to transition out of your personal struggle?

_____

_____

_____

_____

NOTES

Have you been holding in this personal struggle or have you reached out to someone? Why or why not?

_____

_____

_____

_____

What do you do when you find yourself engaging into the personal struggle or if the struggle presents itself to you? *(Do you resist, get angry, give in, scream etc.)*

_____

_____

_____

_____

Has your struggle caused you to be suicidal? If suicide is your struggle how often do you think about it?

_____

_____

Now that you have answered these questions follow these steps:

- Consult God about what you're dealing with
- Break Communication from People Who Are Involved and do not support helping
- Fasting & Praying

- Limit your intake of non-positive Music, TV & Social Media and replace with positive viewing and listening
- When the Personal Struggle Presents itself call it out, expose it & Resist

Example: Anger you will not over take my mind in the name of Jesus. Devil you must flee God has given me a sound mind.

- Learn Scriptures that pertains to your personal struggle *(Use google if you do not know any)*
- Talk to God throughout the day, make conversation establish relationship show him that you are serious about breaking free
- If possible find someone who has struggled with the same thing and has overcame
- PRAY
- Declare every day that you are free in Jesus name

NOTES

2 week follow up:

Have you established a line of communication with God in this 2 week period? Why or Why Not

_____

_____

_____

_____

Were you able to let go of those who mean you no good in this process? Why or Why Not? And if Why not when do you plan on letting them go?

_____

_____

_____

_____

Do you still listen to the same music, watch the same shows less or more? _(Instead of putting thought into when you think you will stop or decrease the limit just start now)_

_____

_____

_____

_____

Are speaking positive to yourself daily? Reading positive words of affirmation? Writing down how you feel?

_____

_____

_____

_____

How has the entire process been the past 2 weeks?

_____

_____

_____

_____

_____

_____

_____

_____

_____

_____

_____

_____

Connect with us we would like to help you in your process

Email us at HLBCDinfo@gmail.com

Be sure to tell us your name

- Mentorship
- Advice
- Questions
- Prayer
- Etc.

www.ingramcontent.com/pod-product-compliance
Lightning Source LLC
Chambersburg PA
CBHW072155090426
42740CB00012B/2281